THE
MONDAY TO
SUNDAY
COOKBOOK

PHOTOGRAPHY BY
CRAIG FRASER

PHILLIPPA CHEIFITZ

THE
MONDAY
TO **SUNDAY**
COOKBOOK

TO MY FAMILY, WHOSE ENTHUSIASM FOR EATING HAS INSPIRED MY COOKING.

With thanks to
Banks
Bright House
Fabric Library
Heartworks
House and Interiors
Latitudes
LIM
Loft Living
Moroccan Warehouse
Rosedene Interiors
Wild Olive

Struik Publishers (a division of New Holland Publishing
(South Africa) (Pty) Ltd)
Cornelis Struik House, 80 McKenzie Street
Cape Town 8001

First published in 2001
1 2 3 4 5 6 7 8 9 10

Publishing manager: Linda de Villiers
Managing editor: Cecilia Barfield
Editor: Brenda Brickman
Designer: Petal Palmer
Design assistant: Natascha Adendorff
Photographer: Craig Fraser
Stylist: Phillippa Cheifitz
Food preparation: Andrea Steer

Reproduction: Hirt & Carter Cape (Pty) Ltd
Printing and binding: Sing Cheong
Printing Company Limited

ISBN 1 86872 624 X

intro**duction**

When Linda de Villiers of Struik Publishers commissioned a new cookbook, I was sure of the format. I wanted a book that would reflect my lifestyle and have a credibility that readers could trust. After years of enthusiastic food writing, my food files are crammed with recipes written for *Cosmopolitan, Femina* and *House and Leisure* magazines. These presented endless possibilities, all equally good. But for this book I have carefully selected the ones that I use the most, as they best suit the way I eat at home: simply with family, or more festively with friends.

Arabella Boxer, a renowned English food writer, once wrote that food shared with guests should be no different to daily fare, there should simply be more of it. I adhere to this strongly, and sincerely hope that the following recipes in this book, with their easy-to-follow, explicit instructions, will provide delicious meals in your home at all times. It takes no less time to provide a bad dish than a good one. Simply relax, pour a glass of wine, listen to your favourite music and enjoy the task.

Today quality and interesting ingredients are widely available. Take pleasure in choosing them. Make the most of the seasonal, selecting recipes accordingly, as this will give you the best value for your spending. If pressed for time, make use of ready-prepared washed and cut vegetables and greens, rather than factory-produced sauces and dressings that overwhelm the flavours of good ingredients. The Italians are happy to simply dress a bowl of greens at table with a squirt of fine vinegar and a dousing of the best olive oil, so why not you? Buying the best oil and vinegar is a better investment than a commercial dressing. And when they come in a well-designed bottle, look a lot prettier. In fact collect the bottles, and fill them with flowers to pretty up the table. Add a green salad and fresh fruit to an easily prepared main course and savour a fine meal at the end of the most hectic working day. Be more generous with your time over a weekend to please friends or family, indulging them with a celebration of a dish and a fabulous dessert.

Serving suggestions are exactly that – suggestions. Appetites differ. The more kilo-conscious, the more the food goes around. But take care when feeding teenagers that there's ample for seconds. If only one course is served, make it plentiful. But if it's part of a three-course dinner, it will go a lot further. That's when 4–6, means six not four.

Customs differ. At the Lebanese table, a hostess doesn't double the dish, but puts out more dishes, meze style. For a Chinese meal, think of making a pot of English tea. The general rule is one dish for each guest plus one extra.

If setting out a variety of foods, buffet style, don't multiply on everything. You'll be amazed at the leftovers. Simply do a count – across the board – and decide how many portions the dishes should serve.

Phillippa Cheifitz

monday suppers easy does it

AFTER A WEEKEND OF INDULGENCE,
I CRAVE BROWN RICE AND VEGETABLES
OR SOMETHING EQUALLY COMFORTING.
I DON'T MIND A QUICK SHOP ON THE WAY
HOME, BUT PREFER TO RELY
ON STORE-CUPBOARD INGREDIENTS
OR LEFTOVER WEEKEND PURCHASES
IN THE REFRIGERATOR.

roasted butternut with goat cheese on mixed-grain pilaf

10

for 6

3 butternut squash, about 500 g each
6 whole unpeeled garlic cloves
fresh thyme sprigs
olive oil
salt and milled black pepper
1 x 125 g cylinder chevin (soft goat cheese)

mixed-grain pilaf
1 onion, thinly sliced
2–3 tablespoons oil
1 clove garlic, crushed
1 cup whole pearled wheat
1 cup brown rice
1 cup lentils
1 cinnamon stick
1 bay leaf
1 teaspoon salt
5 cups vegetable stock or water
salt and milled black pepper

green salad to serve
fresh thyme to garnish

Cut the butternut squash lengthwise and scoop out the seeds. Arrange in an oiled baking tin. Place a garlic clove and some thyme into each halved squash, and moisten with olive oil. Season lightly. Cover with oiled greaseproof paper and bake at 200°C for an hour, or until tender. Remove the paper. Add a slice or two of goat cheese. Return to the oven for about 10 minutes until cheese begins to melt. Garnish with fresh thyme. Serve with mixed-grain pilaf and a green salad on the side.

To make the mixed-grain pilaf, soften the onion in the heated oil in a suitable saucepan. Add the garlic, grains and lentils, and stir until all the grains are well mixed. Add the cinnamon and bay leaf, and pour over stock. Add the teaspoon of salt and bring to a simmer. Cover and cook for 40 minutes or until tender. Adjust seasoning to taste. Any leftovers freeze well.

greek-style **vegetable and feta stew**

for 4

½ cup olive oil
2 onions, thinly sliced
2 sticks celery, thinly sliced
2 cloves garlic, crushed
500 g baby marrows, thickly sliced
250 g carrots, thickly sliced
500 g eggplant, cubed
1 x 410 g tin peeled and diced tomatoes
1 cup vegetable stock
2 tablespoons chopped parsley
1 bay leaf
½ cup olives
1 x 410 g tin butter beans, drained and rinsed
200 g feta, crumbled
½ teaspoon dried origanum
milled black pepper

freshly cooked orzo (rice-shaped pasta)
to serve
basil leaves to garnish

Heat ⅓ cup of the oil in a suitable saucepan. Add the onions and celery and cook gently until softened but not browned. Stir in the garlic and then the baby marrows, carrots and eggplant. Cook for 5 minutes before adding the tomatoes, stock, parsley and bay leaf. Cover and simmer for 20 minutes or until the vegetables are tender. Add the olives, beans, feta, origanum and a grinding of black pepper. Spoon the remaining 2 tablespoons of the olive oil over this mixture, and simmer for another 5 minutes or until all is hot and tender and the cheese is starting to melt.
Serve over freshly cooked orzo scattered with basil leaves.

crunchy slaw with baked potatoes and blue cheese

for 6

A baked potato is the ultimate comfort food. Use large baking potatoes. Slice an X across, rub with olive oil and coarse salt, and bake in the oven for about an hour. If you're absolutely pressed for time, microwave. A friend of mine puts on the oven while microwaving the potatoes, then puts the microwaved potatoes in the oven for about 10 minutes so that they taste more like the real thing.
A quicker option is a dollop of Duetto Blue, a delicious, ready-mixed blend of mascarpone and blue cheese. And if you don't like blue cheese, a slice of ricotta or feta is good too.

6 hot baked potatoes to serve
chives to garnish
2 baby cabbages, finely shredded
crisp lettuce, finely shredded
2 carrots, peeled and cut into strips
2 sticks celery, cut into strips
1 large sweet pepper, cut into strips
4–6 spring onions, cut into strips

dressing
⅔ cup sunflower oil
6 tablespoons apple cider vinegar
drizzle of honey
salt and milled black pepper

blue cheese topping
125 g mascarpone
125 g crumbled blue cheese
milled black pepper

Mix the salad ingredients together with the dressing, and turn onto 6 plates. Add a hot baked potato to each plate.

Mash together the blue cheese topping ingredients.

Slash the potatoes across the top and spoon over the blue cheese topping. Garnish with chives.

braised pumpkin with sage, grilled tomato sauce and cheesy polenta

for 4

2 tablespoons olive oil
1 onion, chopped
2 cloves garlic, crushed
2 tablespoons fresh sage, chopped
1 kg diced pumpkin
salt and milled black pepper
1 cup vegetable stock

grilled tomato sauce
750 g ripe Italian plum tomatoes
olive oil
salt and milled black pepper

polenta
2 cups instant polenta
125 g mascarpone
1 cup grated Italian Parmesan
salt and milled black pepper

shaved Italian Parmesan to serve

To make the pumpkin, heat the oil in a large saucepan and add onion. Gently cook until softened but not browned. Stir in the garlic and sage. Add the pumpkin and seasoning. Cover and cook for about 5 minutes. Pour in the stock and simmer for 20 minutes or until tender.

To make the grilled tomato sauce, arrange the tomatoes on an oiled grill pan and moisten them with oil. Slide under a hot grill for 5–10 minutes or until soft and beginning to char. Purée in a blender or processor. If the sauce is too thin, transfer to a saucepan and reduce over a high heat to a suitable consistency. Season to taste.

Make the polenta according to the instructions on the packet, then whisk in the cheeses. Add seasoning to taste.

toasted barley with pan-grilled mushrooms

for 2 – 4

1½ cups pearl barley
4½ cups vegetable stock
3–4 tablespoons chopped fresh dill
salt and milled black pepper
4 large open brown mushrooms
melted butter

baby greens, and thick sour cream
or crème fraîche to serve

Dry-fry the barley in a large, heavy saucepan, stirring now and again, until pale gold in colour. Pour over the stock, and bring to a simmer. Reduce the heat, cover and simmer for half an hour, or until the barley is tender and the liquid absorbed. Stir in the chopped dill and season to taste.

Brush the mushrooms with melted butter and cook on a hot, ridged cast-iron pan, turning once, until just cooked and still fleshy. Top each serving of barley with a mushroom and a spoonful of cream. Tuck in baby greens.

pan-fried fish with salsa verde

for 6 – 8

Salsa verde keeps well in the refrigerator, and it is also delicious with thinly sliced Italian meats – salami, ham, tongue or mortadella. Served with hot boiled potatoes and a green salad on the side, it makes a quick supper.

4 dressed soles,
or 4 portions fresh fish fillets
flour
1 free-range egg, beaten
salt and pepper
oil for frying

roasted potato wedges
4–6 large potatoes
olive oil for moistening
sprigs of rosemary (optional)
salt and milled black pepper

salsa verde
1 cup chopped Italian parsley
1 clove garlic, crushed
1 small onion, crushed
4 anchovy fillets, chopped
1 tablespoon capers,
   well-rinsed and chopped
1 tablespoon red wine vinegar
⅓–½ cup olive oil
milled black pepper

Wash and dry the fish. Dip the fish in flour, then in seasoned beaten egg, and fry in hot oil until golden brown. Drain well and serve with salsa verde and steamed baby potatoes.

If you have time, **roast the potato wedges.** They're no trouble to make, but they obviously take longer than hob-cooked steamed potatoes. Scrub the potatoes, rinse, pat dry and cut into wedges. Moisten with oil and season. Arrange in a single layer on an oiled baking sheet. If you like, tuck in rosemary. Roast at 230°C for 45–60 minutes, turning 3 or 4 times, until golden and tender.

Make the salsa verde by blending the ingredients together to form a paste.

herbed chickpea burgers with fresh tomato couscous

for 4

500 g mashed, cooked chickpeas,
or 500 g lean minced lamb
1 onion, finely chopped
2 tablespoons olive oil
1 teaspoon ground coriander
1 teaspoon ground cumin
1 clove garlic, crushed
1 egg
2 tablespoons plain yoghurt
1 teaspoon crushed dried mint
½ teaspoon dried origanum
2 tablespoons fresh coriander leaves, chopped
salt and milled pepper
couscous for coating
oil for frying

fresh tomato couscous

250 g instant couscous
1 large onion, chopped
2 tablespoons olive oil
2 cloves garlic, crushed
1 teaspoon coriander seeds, cracked
4 firm ripe red tomatoes, chopped
½ cup black olives
juice of a lemon
½ cup coriander leaves, chopped
salt and milled pepper
fresh tomato couscous and crisp
  baby lettuce leaves to serve

Soften the onion in the heated oil until pale golden. Stir in coriander, cumin, garlic and a little seasoning. Beat egg, yoghurt and a little seasoning, then stir in herbs. Mix this with mashed chickpeas or lamb and cooked onion mixture and add a bit more seasoning. Knead lightly and refrigerate overnight to intensify flavours. Bring back to room temperature before frying. Shape into 4 thick flat patties. Coat with couscous and fry in hot shallow oil until browned on both sides, about 5 minutes a side. Serve with fresh tomato couscous and tuck in crisp baby lettuce leaves.

   To make the fresh tomato couscous, cover the couscous with boiling water and leave for 5–10 minutes or until absorbed, then fluff up with a fork. Meanwhile soften the onion in the heated oil until pale golden. Stir in garlic, coriander seeds and soaked couscous. Add the rest of the ingredients and check seasoning.

cracked pepper steaks with crushed potatoes

for 4

There's nothing that is quicker to make or more delicious to eat than a steak. It doesn't have to be beef: it can be lamb, or even ostrich, which is blissfully healthy. And don't forget fish – a rare tuna steak is a treat.

4 steaks of your choice, about 200 g each
oil
coarsely cracked pepper
milled salt

crushed potatoes
750 g potatoes
chicken or vegetable stock
2–3 tablespoons butter
2–3 tablespoons crème fraîche
salt and milled black pepper

steamed green beans or creamy spinach to serve

Heat a cast-iron pan until really hot. Coat the pan with a non-stick cooking spray to prevent sticking. Oil the steaks (not the pan) and press both sides firmly into the coarsely cracked pepper. Sear the steaks in the really hot pan until well-browned on the outside, but still rare inside. If you wish to cook them longer, slide under a hot grill for a few minutes. Allow to rest, covered, for a few minutes. Salt to taste.

For the crushed potatoes, scrub the potatoes well, or peel if you prefer. Cut the potatoes into chunks and simmer in enough stock to cover, until tender. Pour off the liquid and set aside. Roughly crush the potatoes by hand with a potato masher, adding butter and crème fraîche, and if necessary, a few spoonfuls of reserved broth. Add seasoning to taste.

Serve the steaks with the crushed potatoes and steamed green beans or creamy spinach.

honeyed roast chicken breasts and vegetables

for 4

4 chicken breasts with skin and bone
8 teaspoons soft butter
fresh sage leaves, rinsed and dried
500 g butternut, ready-cubed
500 g sweet potato, ready-cubed
olive oil
2 tablespoons honey
2 tablespoons lemon juice
salt and milled black pepper

sage leaves to garnish

Wash, dry and season the chicken.
Push some butter and 2 or 3 sage leaves under the skin. In an oiled roasting pan, arrange the butternut and sweet potato in a single layer. Season and moisten with olive oil. Top with chicken breasts and roast at 220°C for 20–25 minutes until golden but still moist. Mix honey and lemon juice and spoon over the chicken. Cover, and leave to stand for 5 minutes to glaze. Garnish with sage leaves. Serve immediately.

CHICKEN BREASTS ARE A GOOD OPTION FOR WEEKDAY MEALS, AS THEY COOK IN LESS TIME THAN A WHOLE CHICKEN, BUT STILL PROVIDE A HOMEY, COMFORTING MEAL.

tuesday's great grills

GRILLING IS SUCH A FAST WAY OF GETTING
FOOD ON THE TABLE, AS NOT ONLY IS THE
METHOD QUICK, BUT IT TAKES LITTLE TIME
FOR THE GRILL TO GET TO THE FIERCE
TEMPERATURE REQUIRED.
ON A BALMY SUMMER EVENING, PERHAPS
YOU CAN PERSUADE A PARTNER TO
PREPARE A FIRE OUTSIDE, AS NOTHING
BEATS A BARBECUE.

TUESDAY

grilled fish in coriander oil with avocado sauce

for 4 – 6

500–700 g filleted fish, cut into chunks
1 cup coriander leaves
⅓ cup olive oil
salt and milled black pepper

avocado sauce

1–2 large ripe avocados
1–2 tablespoons lemon or lime juice
1–2 small chillies, deseeded and chopped
2–4 tablespoons chopped coriander leaves
salt

basmati rice to serve

Soak some short, thin bamboo skewers in water for about an hour. Blanch the coriander leaves in boiling water for 10 seconds, then drain and dry well. Blend the coriander leaves together with the oil. Mix with the chunks of fish, adding some seasoning. Thread one piece of fish onto each skewer. Slide under a hot preheated grill and cook quickly until just done and still moist. Serve the grilled fish with the avocado sauce and hot, steamed basmati rice.

For the avocado sauce, mash together all the ingredients.

BLANCH THE CORIANDER
SO THAT IT KEEPS ITS
BRIGHT GREEN COLOUR.

grilled fish with parsley and goat cheese pesto and mashed sweet potatoes

25

for 6

Use any fish, as long as it is very fresh.

6 portions fresh fish, about 250 g each, skinned and filleted
salt
olive oil

parsley and peppered goat cheese pesto

50 g fresh Italian parsley, chopped
3 cloves garlic, crushed
¼ cup roasted sunflower seeds
⅔ cup olive oil
125 g peppered, soft goat cheese
salt

mashed sweet potatoes

1 kg sweet potatoes, peeled and cut into chunks
¾ cup orange juice
2 tablespoons butter
grated nutmeg
salt and milled black pepper

Italian parsley to garnish

Wash and lightly salt the fish. Leave for half an hour at room temperature or refrigerate if leaving longer. Rinse and pat dry. Brush with oil and place in a single layer in a well-oiled baking tin. Slide under a searing hot grill until just cooked and still moist. Remove from the oven. Top the fish with the pesto and serve with mashed sweet potatoes.

For the pesto, process the parsley, garlic, seeds and oil to form a paste. Blend or mash in the cheese. Add a little salt if needed.

Cook the potatoes in salted water for 20–30 minutes or until tender right through. Drain, reserving the cooking water, and return the potatoes to the hot saucepan. Return the saucepan to the turned-off hob. Cover with a lid and leave for a few minutes. Gradually mash in the juice and butter, adding some of the reserved water if necessary. Add nutmeg and seasoning to taste.

grilled yellowtail with tomato and basil dressing

for 4 – 6

4–6 yellowtail steaks
½ cup good olive oil
¼ cup shredded basil leaves
2 tablespoons lemon juice
3 spring onions, chopped
6 ripe red tomatoes, skinned and chopped

2 fat cloves garlic, crushed
salt and milled black pepper

steamed potatoes to serve
sprigs of basil to garnish

Season the fish and moisten with some of the oil. Mix the remaining ingredients together, seasoning to taste. Slide the fish under a hot grill or over hot coals and cook for a few minutes each side until just cooked and still moist. Remove to a platter and pour over the tomato and basil dressing. Garnish with sprigs of basil and serve immediately. It's very good with steamed potatoes on the side.

grilled red fish with citrus

for 4

2 small whole red fish, about 750 g each,
separated into 4 large fillets
olive oil for brushing
salt and milled black pepper

citrus sauce

shredded rind of 1 bright lemon, blanched
shredded rind of 1 bright orange, blanched
⅔ cup fresh lemon juice
½ cup fresh orange juice
3 tablespoons runny honey
chunk of ginger, crushed
½ cup cream

segments of ruby grapefruit and orange, and
fresh herbs to garnish

Season and oil the fish fillets, then grill until just firm to the touch.

To make the citrus sauce, bring the citrus rinds, juices and honey to the boil. Add the ginger and cream and boil vigorously to emulsify. Check the seasoning and also the sweet-sour balance and adjust if necessary.

Spoon the citrus sauce over the fish, and garnish with segments of orange and grapefruit, and fresh herbs.

grilled calamari salad

for 6

6 cleaned calamari, about 1 kg
olive oil for moistening

dressing

½ cup olive oil
¼ cup fresh lemon juice
2 cloves garlic, crushed
2 red chillies, chopped
salt and milled black pepper

salad

1 cos lettuce
1 butter lettuce
3 tomatoes, cut into wedges
6 small crisp cucumbers, sliced lengthwise
100 g feta, cubed
handful of Calamata olives
sprinkling of dried origanum

Cut the calamari in half, lengthwise. Wash and dry well. Score on the inside in a criss-cross pattern. Moisten with olive oil. Arrange in a single layer on a grill pan, cooking the calamari in two batches if necessary.

Make the dressing by mixing together all the ingredients.

Slide the calamari under a very hot grill and sear for a minute or two until opaque, just cooked and starting to curl. Turn with tongs and grill for barely a minute on the other side. Overcooking will toughen the calamari. Immediately pour over the dressing.

For the salad, arrange the washed and dried lettuce leaves in a salad bowl. Add the grilled calamari and dressing. Add the rest of the salad ingredients and moisten with a little olive oil; season to taste.

penne with grilled vegetable sauce

for 4 – 6

400 g freshly cooked penne

grilled vegetables

1 small aubergine,
sliced lengthways
1 red and yellow pepper,
sliced lengthways
350–400 g baby marrows,
halved lengthways
3 tablespoons olive oil
1 tablespoon balsamic vinegar

tomatoes

2 x 410 g tins tomatoes, crushed
1 or 2 fat cloves garlic, crushed
1 teaspoon dried origanum
pinch sugar (if needed)
¼ cup cream (optional)
salt and milled black pepper
shredded basil leaves or chopped
Italian parsley

grated Italian Parmesan to serve

For the grilled vegetables, preheat the grill. Brush a baking sheet the size of the grill with olive oil. Spread the vegetables in a single layer on the baking sheet. Season, then moisten with olive oil. Turning halfway, grill the vegetables for about 10 minutes, until tender and starting to char. Dress with the olive oil and vinegar. Add basil or parsley.

Meantime, on top of the stove, **reduce the tomatoes** with the garlic, origanum and a little seasoning for about 10 minutes. Taste to check seasoning and tartness, and adjust if necessary. If you like, add a little cream and heat through.

Mix the tomato with the drained pasta, and top with the grilled vegetables and lots of Parmesan.

GRILLED VEGETABLES ARE QUICK TO PREPARE AND MAKE A HEALTHY, CHUNKY PASTA SAUCE WHEN MIXED WITH TOMATOES REDUCED ON TOP OF THE STOVE.

grilled butterflied chicken with rosemary oil

for 2 – 4

1 small whole free-range chicken,
about 1 kg
olive oil
salt and milled black pepper

rosemary oil
½ cup olive oil
¼ cup fresh rosemary sprigs

steamed new potatoes and
baby leaf greens
to serve
lemon wedges to garnish

Use a pair of kitchen scissors to remove the backbone and wingtips (freeze for broth). Wash and dry the chicken well. Flatten the chicken with the heel of your hand. Rub with olive oil and season. Slide under a hot but not fierce grill, skin-side down and low enough to avoid burning. Grill for about 15 minutes, then turn skin-side up and grill for another 10–15 minutes, or until the skin is crisp and golden and the flesh is just cooked.

Prepare the rosemary oil by gently heating the oil and rosemary in a small but heavy saucepan. Simmer very gently for a few minutes until the rosemary starts to crisp. Remove and cool, then strain. Use at room temperature.

Cut the chicken into 2–4 portions, and place on hot plates. Immediately spoon over a little rosemary oil and garnish with lemon wedges. Serve with steamed new potatoes and baby leaf greens.

grilled marinated lamb chops
with grilled onions and mixed mash

for 4 – 6

12 lamb rib chops, trimmed

marinade

1 tablespoon whole-grain mustard
4 tablespoons balsamic vinegar
⅓ cup olive oil
salt and milled black pepper

grilled onions

2–4 onions, sliced fairly thickly
olive oil
balsamic vinegar

mixed mash

250 g potatoes, peeled and cubed
250 g parsnips, peeled and cubed
250 g carrots or pumpkin, peeled and cubed
50 g butter
½ cup cream
salt and milled black pepper
grated nutmeg

chopped chives to garnish

First make the marinade by mixing together the marinade ingredients. Marinate the chops overnight in the refrigerator, or simply while heating the grill. Make sure that they are at room temperature for cooking. Arrange the chops on the grill pan, fat side up, and grill until crisp and brown. Then grill on both sides until nicely browned outside but still rare inside.

To make the grilled onions, moisten them with a little oil. Spread as flat as possible in a single layer on an oiled grill pan. Slide under a hot grill and cook for approximately 10 minutes, turning once or twice, until tender and starting to char. Remove from the grill and flavour sparingly with balsamic vinegar and a little seasoning.

To make the mixed mash, simmer the vegetables in boiling water with a little salt, for about 20 minutes or until tender. Pour off the water and return to the stove to dry. Add the butter and cream and heat through. Mash roughly by hand with a potato masher, adding seasoning and nutmeg to taste. Garnish with chives.

grilled lamb sausage with fruit and vegetable couscous

for 6 – 8

1 kg lamb sausage

vegetables and broth
1 bunch carrots, scraped and thickly sliced
1 x 400 g tin chickpeas, rinsed and drained
500 g pumpkin chunks
250–500 g whole baby marrows
1 large onion, sliced
2 sticks cinnamon
2 teaspoons ground coriander
1 teaspoon ground cumin
1 fresh chilli, chopped

5 cups water or chicken broth
handful of coriander leaves
salt and pepper

fruit and vegetable couscous
2 cups couscous (wholewheat if available)
½ cup chopped dried figs
½ cup chopped dried apricots

½ cup toasted pumpkin seeds, and fresh
   coriander leaves to garnish
African Nali sauce or any hot chilli sauce
   to serve

First make the broth by simmering together all the ingredients for about 45 minutes. Check seasoning. Strain. Keep the vegetables warm.

Make the couscous by pouring 3 cups of the boiling-hot broth over the couscous. Stir in the chopped dried fruits. Allow to stand for 5–10 minutes until the liquid has been absorbed and the grains are tender. If they're not, simply add a little more boiling liquid.

Cook the sausage under a preheated grill until nicely browned but still juicy.

Fluff up the hot couscous with a fork and pile onto a platter. Top with the vegetables, chunks of grilled sausage, toasted pumpkin seeds and coriander leaves, and serve. Reheat the remaining broth to serve on the side.

wednesday's meals-in-one

IN WINTER THERE'S NOTHING MORE SATISFYING THAN
A BIG BOWL OF HOT SOUP, A VERITABLE MEAL ON
ITS OWN. OR A SUBSTANTIAL SALAD ON A WARM DAY,
WHILE PASTA COMFORTS WHATEVER THE SEASON.
LEFTOVER SOUPS AND PASTAS FREEZE WELL, BUT DO
SO IN SINGLE PORTIONS, TO QUICKLY MICROWAVE
WHEN THERE'S NO TIME TO COOK.

WEDNESDAY

sweet potato and ginger soup with chorizo

for 4

1 bunch spring onions, trimmed and chopped

2 tablespoons sunflower oil

2–3 tablespoons chopped peeled fresh ginger

1 fresh green chilli, chopped

1 kg sweet potatoes, peeled and cubed

3 cups chicken stock

1 x 400 ml tin coconut milk

½ cup chopped coriander leaves

salt and milled black pepper to taste

about 250 g pan-grilled chorizo slices, and coriander leaves to serve

Gently soften the onions in the heated oil. Stir in the ginger and chilli. Add the cubed sweet potatoes and a little seasoning. Cover and leave to absorb the flavours gently for 5–10 minutes. Pour in the stock and coconut milk. Cover and simmer for 20–30 minutes, or until the potatoes are very tender. Purée and check seasoning. Stir in the chopped coriander leaves.

Top with pan-grilled sausage slices and a few coriander leaves.

THE COOKING TIME, AND NOT NECESSARILY THE PREPARATION OF SOUP IS OFTEN LONG, BUT SOUPS CAN BE PREPARED AN EVENING IN ADVANCE. STANDING OVERNIGHT IN THE REFRIGERATOR WILL ONLY IMPROVE THE FLAVOUR, AND IT'S GREAT TO HAVE THE MEAL READY TO HEAT IF YOU COME HOME LATE.

tuscan-style **vegetable and bread soup**

for 8

250 g dried white beans
⅓ cup olive oil
125 g pancetta, chopped
1 large onion, chopped
500 g baby marrows, chopped
3 sticks celery, chopped
1 large carrot, chopped
2 cloves garlic, crushed
1 x 410 g tin tomatoes, crushed
½ cup basil leaves, shredded
4 cups shredded cabbage
2 cups shredded Swiss chard
salt and milled black pepper

oven-toasted ciabatta
8 slices ciabatta bread
1 head garlic, halved

shavings of Italian Parmesan and
good olive oil to serve

Soak the beans overnight, drain and simmer, covered with water, for an hour. Heat the oil in a large, heavy saucepan and add the pancetta, onion, baby marrows, celery, carrot and a little seasoning. Cook gently until softened but still pale in colour. Stir in the garlic, then the tomato, basil, cabbage, Swiss chard and some seasoning and simmer for 10 minutes. Drain the beans, but keep the cooking liquid. Purée half the beans and return to the pot together with the rest of the whole beans. Measure the bean cooking liquid and add 8 cups to the soup. If necessary add stock to make up the required liquid. Add seasoning to taste.

Toast the sliced ciabatta at 180°C for 10 minutes or until pale golden. Rub with halved garlic.

To serve, place a slice of toasted bread in each large soup bowl. Ladle over the hot soup. Add shavings of Parmesan and a drizzle of olive oil.

vegetable **pot-au-feu**

for 6

roasted vegetable broth
1 large onion
250 g white button mushrooms
3 or 4 carrots
2 or 3 parsnips
2 or 3 turnips
1 or 2 sticks celery
4 fat cloves garlic, smashed
1–2 tablespoons olive oil
salt and milled black pepper
8 cups water
1 cup coarsely shredded spinach
1 or 2 chopped leeks
¼ cup chopped parsley
few sprigs fresh thyme

1 bay leaf
1 teaspoon salt and a few peppercorns

vegetable chunks
1.5 kg assorted mixed vegetables:
baby cabbage wedges
baby carrots
chunks of parsnip
chunks or slices of pumpkin
wedges of turnip
halved baby squash
florets of cauliflower

freshly grated Parmesan to serve

For broth, wash, peel and trim the onions, mushrooms, carrots, parsnips, turnips and celery, then chop roughly. Turn into an oiled roasting pan with the garlic, and moisten with olive oil. Season lightly. Roast at 200°C for 40 minutes, stirring now and again, or until soft. Stir in 2 cups water, scraping up any browned bits. Turn into a saucepan, add remaining 6 cups water, spinach, leeks, herbs and a little seasoning. Bring to a boil, reduce the heat and simmer, covered, for about half an hour. Strain and check seasoning. If you like, freeze these vegetables to add bulk to some other stew or soup.

For the vegetable chunks, simmer the vegetables in the strained broth until tender.

To serve, dish up the cooked vegetable chunks into 6 large soup bowls. At the table, pour over the hot, strained broth. Pass around freshly grated Italian Parmesan.

tomato, chickpea and orzo soup

for 4

1 onion, chopped
1 carrot, chopped
1 cup chopped celery
3 tablespoons olive oil
3 tablespoons chopped parsley
1 teaspoon dried origanum
2 cloves garlic, crushed
2 x 410 g tins tomatoes, crushed
¼ cup sundried tomato pesto
3 cups chicken or vegetable stock
2 cups cooked or tinned chickpeas
2 cups cooked orzo
(simmer in stock for extra flavour)
salt and milled black pepper

basil oil
a bunch of basil leaves
½ cup good olive oil

grated Italian Parmesan to garnish

Gently soften the onion, carrot and celery in the heated oil, covered, for about 10 minutes. Add a little salt and pepper, and the parsley and origanum, and cook very gently, covered, for 5–10 minutes. Stir in the garlic and cook for another minute or two. Add the tomatoes and more seasoning, and simmer for about 10 minutes. Add the pesto and stock and simmer for about 20 minutes. Add the chickpeas and simmer for a further 10 minutes. Add the cooked pasta and heat through. Check seasoning.

To make the basil oil, blend together the olive oil and washed and dried, torn basil leaves.

Serve the soup drizzled with basil oil and sprinkled with Parmesan.

chopped **roasted vegetable salad**

for 6 – 8

1.5 kg mix of vegetables:
halved sweet peppers
halved peeled onions
halved aubergines
whole baby marrows
wedges of pumpkin or chunks of butternut
whole garlic cloves, unpeeled
2 corn cobs
olive oil
sprigs of fresh thyme

dressing
⅓ cup freshly squeezed lime juice
(or lemon juice)
roasted garlic cloves
½–¾ cup good olive oil
salt and milled black pepper

shredded greens or a mix of
baby greens to serve

Slice the corn off the cob. Chop the remaining vegetables, peeling or skinning where necessary.

Moisten the vegetables with olive oil and arrange in a single layer in one or more oiled roasting pans. Tuck in thyme. Roast at 220°C for 45 minutes or until tender and starting to catch at the edges.

Make a dressing with the lime juice by mixing it with the oil. Season to taste, and add as much of the roasted garlic, mashed and peeled, as you prefer.

Just before serving, mix the vegetables and dressing with shredded greens, or spoon onto a mix of baby greens.

THESE SALADS ARE ENOUGH FOR A MEAL ON THEIR OWN, BUT THEY WILL, OF COURSE, FEED A LOT MORE PEOPLE IF YOU WISH TO SERVE THEM AS A STARTER ON ANOTHER OCCASION.

tabbouleh with lettuce, baked feta and pita

for 4

1 cup bulgur or cracked wheat
3 medium, firm red tomatoes, seeded and chopped
1 bunch spring onions, chopped
250 g small, crisp cucumbers, chopped
1 cup fresh herbs, chopped (any mix of Italian parsley, mint, coriander and dill)
2–3 tablespoons olive oil
2–3 tablespoons lemon juice
salt and milled black pepper
1 cos lettuce, washed and separated into leaves

baked feta

4 rounds of feta
1 tablespoon olive oil
1 tablespoon oregano leaves, chopped or ½ teaspoon dried origanum
1 clove garlic, crushed
milled black pepper

warm pita breads to serve

Pour boiling water over the wheat and leave to stand for 20 minutes. Drain well. Mix the wheat together with the chopped ingredients, oil and lemon juice and season to taste. Spoon into 4 bowls. Add lettuce leaves for scooping.

To make the baked feta, place the feta rounds on a sheet of greaseproof paper. Add the rest of the ingredients and wrap up, twisting the ends. Place in a suitable dish and bake at 180°C for 10–15 minutes or until soft. Drain any excess liquid and drizzle with a little more oil, if you like.

Top the salad with warm, baked feta, and serve with warm pita breads.

44

african **caesar salad**

for 4

2 cos lettuces
1 large avocado
long shavings of moist biltong
75–100 g shavings of Italian Parmesan

garlic croutons
day old white bread
about ½ cup olive oil
1–2 cloves garlic, crushed

dressing
1 free-range egg
3 tablespoons lemon juice
2 teaspoons Dijon mustard
⅓ cup olive oil
salt and milled black pepper

IF YOU DON'T WISH TO
INCLUDE BILTONG IN
THIS SALAD, SUBSTITUTE
WITH EXTRA AVOCADO.

To make the garlic croutons, break off irregular pieces of bread, discarding the crust, to make 2–3 cups. Gently heat the olive oil with the crushed garlic until aromatic, then allow to cool. Toss the bread in just enough of the oil to moisten it, then bake in a single layer at 180°C for 10 minutes or until golden and crisp. Strain off any leftover oil and use to make up the oil required for the dressing.

To make the dressing, place the egg in boiling water for 1 minute, then remove. Shell the coddled egg and blend with the lemon juice, mustard and a little seasoning. Add the oil and check seasoning, but remember that both the biltong and the cheese are salty.

To serve, wash and dry the lettuce leaves. Slice the avocado. Mix the lettuce and avocado with half the dressing and turn into a salad bowl or onto 4 plates. Add biltong, Parmesan and garlic croutons. Drizzle the rest of the dressing over the salad and add a grinding of black pepper. Serve immediately.

red salad with beetroot and seared beef

for 6

8 medium beetroot
2 x 250 g chunks of beef fillet
oil
coarsely ground black pepper
or 2 cylinders peppered chevin (in place
of the beef, oil and pepper)

1 red lettuce
1 head radicchio (or another red lettuce)
1 white or red onion, thinly sliced
1 baby red cabbage, shredded
250 g small potatoes, halved

mustard vinaigrette
½ cup olive oil
2 tablespoons red wine vinegar
1 tablespoon balsamic vinegar
2 teaspoons Dijon mustard
1 clove garlic, crushed
1 teaspoon honey
2 tablespoons chopped parsley
salt and milled black pepper to taste

shreds of red spring onion or chives to garnish

Scrub the beetroot and bake at 200°C for an hour or until tender. Allow to cool, then skin and cut into slim wedges.

Moisten the steaks with oil and roll in coarsely ground black pepper. Sear the beef all over in a heavy non-stick pan until well browned but still rare. Allow to rest for half an hour before slicing very thinly. Or, if you are using chevin, slice the goat cheese.

Prepare the dressing by mixing together all the ingredients.

Mix the sliced beef together with a quarter of the dressing.

Wash and dry the salad leaves and mix with the rest of the dressing or all of the dressing if you are not using beef. Turn onto a platter and top with the beetroot and beef, or beetroot and chevin. Add the onion and cabbage.

Steam the potatoes until tender and, while still warm, add to the salad platter. Add a grinding of salt if needed. Garnish with spring onions or chives.

angel hair pasta with lettuce and basil cream sauce

for 4

2 crisp medium lettuces
4 tablespoons olive oil
1 cup chicken or vegetable stock
1 cup cream
30 g basil leaves, torn
1 clove garlic, crushed
grated zest of 1 lemon, blanched
salt and milled black pepper
500 g angel-hair pasta, freshly cooked

shaved Parmesan and olive oil to serve

Wash the whole lettuces and drain. Thump, stem side down on the cutting board and remove the loosened cores. Slice into wedges. Heat the olive oil in a suitable saucepan. Add the lettuce wedges and stock. Cover and cook for 5 minutes or until just wilted. Blend the cream with the basil and garlic. Simmer together with the lemon rind for a few minutes until lightly thickened. Season to taste and mix with the freshly cooked, drained pasta. Add the lettuce and stock. Mix together and serve immediately, topped with shavings of Parmesan and a drizzle of olive oil.

BRAISED LETTUCE, THE BASIS FOR THIS DISH, CAN BE SERVED AS A VEGETABLE OR TURNED INTO A SOUP BY SIMPLY USING MORE STOCK AND ENRICHING IT WITH A LITTLE CREAM.

penne with spare-rib ragout

for 6

500 g penne, freshly cooked

ragout
1.5 kg spare-ribs
¼ cup olive oil
2 onions, thinly sliced
2 fat cloves garlic, crushed
1 teaspoon dried origanum
1 cup dry red wine
2 x 410 g tins chopped tomatoes
2 tablespoons tomato paste
salt and milled black pepper

Cut each sheet of ribs into 3 or 4 pieces. Heat the olive oil in a heavy casserole. Add the meat and fry until nicely browned. Remove with a slotted spoon and season lightly. Add the onions and cook gently until softened and pale golden in colour. Stir in the garlic and origanum, then pour in the wine and bring the sauce to a fierce bubble. Add the tomatoes and tomato paste, the reserved ribs and some seasoning. Reduce the heat, cover and simmer very gently, stirring now and again, for about an hour and a half or until the meat is very tender and the tomatoes are reduced to a rich sauce. Turn the ribs around from time to time and, if necessary, add a little water now and again. Mix the just cooked, drained pasta with some of the ragout and sprinkle with herbs. Pass around the rest of the sauce and the Parmesan.

baked pasta with butternut squash and tomato-curry sauce

for 6

1 kg butternut squash, in chunks, steamed
500 g short pasta, freshly cooked
1 cup cream
¼ cup coriander leaves
salt and milled black pepper

tomato-curry sauce
2 tablespoons sunflower oil
2 cloves garlic, crushed
2 teaspoons curry powder
2 x 410 g tins chopped tomatoes
sugar (optional)
salt and milled black pepper

topping
1 cup grated Cheddar
½ cup fresh wholewheat crumbs
30 g butter

Gently heat the oil, stir in the garlic, then the curry powder and cook, stirring, for barely a minute. Add the tomatoes and some seasoning, and stir well. Bring to a boil, then reduce the heat and cook gently, stirring now and again, for about 20 minutes. Check seasoning and if necessary, add a pinch sugar.

To assemble, mix the steamed squash with the cooked pasta, cream, coriander and seasoning. Turn into a buttered baking dish. Pour over the tomato-curry sauce and sprinkle with the cheese mixed with the crumbs. Dot with the butter and bake at 190°C for about 30 minutes, or until piping hot and golden in colour.

DEFINITELY A DISH TO PREPARE THE DAY BEFORE. BRING TO ROOM TEMPERATURE WHILE HEATING THE OVEN.

goat cheese macaroni with roasted tomato sauce

for 4

250 g elbow macaroni, freshly cooked

goat cheese sauce
butter
¼ cup flour
2 cups hot milk
grated nutmeg
1 teaspoon dry mustard
125 g soft goat cheese
125 g firm goat cheese, grated
salt and milled black pepper

roasted tomato sauce
16 ripe red tomatoes, skinned and halved
sprigs of thyme, rosemary and basil leaves
6–8 whole, unpeeled garlic cloves
sugar (optional)
about ¼ cup olive oil
milled sea salt and black pepper

freshly grated Parmesan and shredded basil
leaves or chopped Italian parsley to serve

Cook and drain the macaroni. Melt 60 g butter and stir in the flour. Stir continuously until smooth. Gradually stir in the hot milk and cook, stirring, until thick and smooth. Add salt, pepper and nutmeg to taste. Stir in the mustard and the soft goat cheese and stir until melted. Mix together with the well-drained macaroni and turn into a buttered baking dish. Sprinkle with the grated goat cheese and dot with butter. Bake at 200°C for about half an hour or until golden and bubbly.

To make the roasted tomato sauce, place the tomatoes, cut side up, in a single layer, in a large, oiled, shallow baking pan. Tuck in herbs and garlic. Season and, if you like, sprinkle with a little sugar. Moisten generously with olive oil. Roast at 200°C for an hour, or until the tomatoes start to catch and caramelise. If more convenient, roast at 180°C for 1½ hours. Discard the rosemary and thyme stalks, but blend the tomatoes with the thyme leaves, basil and squeezed roasted garlic. Check seasoning.

Serve the macaroni with the hot roasted tomato sauce, and garnish with basil or Italian parsley.

THUR

thursday's pan-asian kitchen

ASIAN TASTES, FROM JAPANESE SUSHI TO THAI CURRIES, HAVE INVADED THE WEST. INGREDIENTS ARE READILY AVAILABLE, NOT ONLY IN SPECIALITY SHOPS BUT IN EVERY SUPERMARKET. GET FAMILIAR WITH THEM AND USE THEM IN THESE UNINTIMIDATING RECIPES, ALL DELICIOUSLY ADDICTIVE. FRESH FRUIT IS THE WAY TO END THE MEAL IN THE EAST: SEGMENTS OF ORANGE TO SUCK AT THE END OF A CHINESE MEAL, OR DAINTY WEDGES OF WATERMELON COMMONLY SERVED AT JAPANESE RESTAURANTS. ALTERNATIVELY, TRY SLICED MANGO, PAPINO OR MELON, MOISTENED WITH ORANGE JUICE, AND FLAVOURED WITH CHOPPED FRESH AND PRESERVED GINGER.

vietnamese fresh **spring rolls**

for 6 – 8

150–200 g fresh bean sprouts
¼ English cucumber
1 carrot, peeled
150–200 g small prawns, cooked and shelled
⅓–½ cup coriander leaves
24–30 small rice paper rounds (about 16 cm in diameter)

nuoc man dipping sauce
1 tablespoon fish sauce
3 tablespoons lime (or lemon) juice
1 clove garlic, finely chopped
1 fresh red chilli, finely chopped
½ teaspoon sugar

peanut sauce
¼ cup hoisin sauce
¼ cup water
1 tablespoon fish sauce
2 tablespoons ground dry-roasted unsalted peanuts
1 fresh red chilli, finely chopped

butter lettuce leaves (optional) to serve

Blanch the sprouts for 1 minute in boiling water. Drain and plunge into ice-cold water. Cut the cucumber and carrot into matchsticks. Mix vegetables with the prawns and coriander leaves. Brush the rice paper rounds lightly with warm water on both sides and leave for 20 seconds. Place a mound of mixture in the centre of each. Fold over the sides, then roll up. Refrigerate until serving.

For the dipping sauces, mix together all the ingredients.

Dip into one of the sauces before eating. If you like, wrap in a soft butter lettuce leaf before dipping.

THIS IS A PRETTY STANDARD FILLING, SO DO FEEL FREE TO DO YOUR OWN THING. MY DAUGHTER'S FRIEND, WHO IS A REMARKABLY GOOD COOK, USES A FILLING OF SHREDDED CHICKEN, MANGO, GINGER AND CORIANDER.

56

miso soups

Makes 2 large or 4 small servings

2 teaspoons dashi broth granules

2 cups boiling water

2 tablespoons miso

what to add

chopped spring onions

wakame seaweed (only a little as it expands
miraculously after simmering
for a few minutes)

blanched sliced tenderstem broccoli
or mangetouts

sliced fresh mushrooms or braised shiitake

cooked noodles (thin wheat or soba
or fat udon)

paper-thin slices of raw fish

cooked peeled prawns

paper-thin slices of chicken fillet (briefly
cooked in the plain broth)

cubes of tofu or deep-fried tofu
tempura

To reconstitute the dashi broth, add boiling water to the granules. To turn into a miso soup, mix the miso to a paste with a little of the dashi broth, then whisk in the rest of the heated broth. Heat through, but never boil.

Add any or all of the suggested ingredients. Weigh down a cake of tofu for about 30 minutes to squeeze out liquid, then slice and coat with cornflour. Deep-fry in hot oil until golden.

A SIMPLE MISO SOUP IS SERVED FOR BREAKFAST, OR AS AN ACCOMPANIMENT TO SUSHI, OR IT CAN BE A VERITABLE MEAL, CHUNKY WITH NOODLES, VEGETABLES AND EVEN TEMPURA. DASHI BROTH, THE CORNERSTONE OF THE JAPANESE KITCHEN, COMES IN INSTANT FREEZE-DRIED GRANULES. USE WHICHEVER MISO YOU PREFER, WHITE OR DARK.

scattered **sushi**

for 2

vinegared sushi rice
1 cup short-grain sushi rice
2–2¼ tablespoons Japanese rice vinegar
1 tablespoon sugar
½–1 teaspoon salt

what to add
pickled ginger
strips of toasted nori (seaweed)
fresh sprouts
blanched mangetouts or sliced tenderstem
broccoli or tatsoi
diagonally sliced cucumber or shredded
daikon radish
braised shiitake mushrooms
strips of grilled chicken
raw or smoked sliced fish
cooked prawns
umeboshi (salty pickled plums)

wasabi paste, Japanese soy to serve
simple miso soup as an accompaniment

Wash rice well and drain. Place in a saucepan with 1⅓ cups water and leave to soak for 30 minutes, then bring to the boil and cook rapidly for a minute. Cover tightly, reduce heat and simmer for 10 minutes. Remove from heat and leave to stand for 10 minutes, still covered.

To make the vinegar mixture, heat the Japanese rice vinegar with the sugar and salt until the sugar has dissolved. Allow to cool.

Turn the cooked rice into a large, shallow dish and gradually fold – never stir – the vinegar mixture into the rice. Cool as quickly as possible. Serve wasabi on the side or fold it into the rice. Serve topped with any of the suggested ingredients.

THIS IS ONE OF THE
EASIEST WAYS OF
SERVING SUSHI.

baked mushrooms and tofu on brown rice with sprouts and chinese greens

for 4

4 large open brown mushrooms
4 squares tofu, about 100 g each
2 tablespoons soy sauce
2 tablesoons balsamic vinegar
1–2 cloves garlic, crushed
1 chunk ginger, peeled and crushed
6–8 slim spring onions
peanut oil

braised Chinese greens
500 g Chinese greens
2 tablespoons peanut oil
1 clove garlic, crushed
1 chunk ginger, peeled and chopped
1 red chilli, seeded and chopped
1 tablespoon soy sauce
¼ to ½ cup chicken stock
sesame oil for sprinkling

steamed brown rice and fresh sprouts to serve

Clean the mushrooms and moisten with oil. Arrange in a single layer together with the tofu in a roasting pan oiled with peanut oil. Mix together the soy, vinegar, garlic and ginger and pour over the mushrooms and tofu. Add the spring onions, trimmed but left whole. Bake at 230°C for 15–20 minutes or until the mushrooms are just done and still fleshy.

Depending on the mix or choice of greens, chop roughly or halve lengthwise or leave small leaves whole. Wash and dry well. Heat the oil with the garlic, ginger and chilli until fragrant. Add the greens, stir around, then pour in the soy and stock. Cover and cook for 5 minutes or until tender but crisp. Drizzle with a little sesame oil.

Serve the mushrooms with brown rice and braised Chinese greens, garnished with sprouts.

tuna teriyaki with stir-fried lettuce

for 4

4 portions skinned and filleted tuna,
about 125 g each

marinade
2 tablespoons Japanese soy sauce
2 tablespoons sake (or dry sherry)
2 tablespoons mirin (or sweet sherry)
1 teaspoon sugar

sauce
2 tablespoons sesame oil
4 spring onions, chopped
1 chunk fresh ginger, peeled and chopped

stir-fried lettuce
1–2 tablespoons peanut oil for frying
1 large crisp lettuce, shredded

steamed rice to serve
shredded daikon radish or fresh sprouts to
garnish

Make the teriyaki marinade by heating together the soy, sake, mirin and sugar until the sugar dissolves. Allow to cool, then pour over the tuna and leave for half an hour.

Remove the tuna from the marinade (reserving the marinade) and roast in an oiled baking pan at 230°C for 4 minutes, turning once, until just done and still moist. Alternatively, sear in a pan.

Heat the sesame oil and stir-fry the onions and ginger until just wilted. Add the reserved marinade and reduce until slightly syrupy.

Stir-fry the lettuce in peanut oil until wilted. Spoon onto 4 plates, top with the tuna and sauce. Garnish with shredded radish or sprouts. Serve with plain, hot, fragrant rice on the side.

thai-style **butternut and fresh salmon soup**

for 4

1 onion, chopped
2 tablespoons sunflower oil
1 red chilli, chopped (or more if you like it hotter)
2 stalks fresh lemongrass, crushed and chopped
1 clove garlic, crushed
500 g peeled and cubed butternut squash
3 cups fish or chicken stock
1 x 400 ml tin coconut cream
3 tablespoons fish sauce

400 g fresh salmon, skinned and filleted
sunflower oil
soy sauce
handful of coriander leaves
salt to taste

200 g Thai rice noodles, freshly cooked
carrot and celery curls and celery leaves to garnish

fish sauce to serve

Gently soften the onion with a little salt in the heated oil, covered, for about 5 minutes. Stir in the chilli, lemongrass and garlic. Add the squash and cook, covered, for about 5 minutes. Pour in the stock and coconut cream and simmer for about 20 minutes or until the squash is very tender. Stir in the fish sauce. Purée until almost smooth. Check seasoning and if required add more fish sauce or salt to taste. If necessary, thin down with more stock. Meanwhile sear the lightly oiled fish on both sides in a heavy ridged pan on top of the stove. Moisten with a little soy sauce and allow to cool for a few minutes. Separate into large chunks. Reheat the soup with a handful of coriander leaves.

To serve, pile noodles in the centre of each large soup bowl. Add fish. Ladle over soup and garnish with carrot and celery curls and leaves. Serve with chopsticks for the noodles and salmon, and soup spoons for the broth. Pass around the fish sauce.

To make carrot and celery curls, use a vegetable peeler, then soak the strips in iced water.

stir-fried calamari with citrus sauce and chilli-peanut noodles

for 2

350 g calamari rings
2 tablespoons peanut oil
1 chunk ginger, peeled and finely chopped
1 fat clove garlic, peeled and finely chopped
2–3 spring onions, chopped

sauce
1 teaspoon cornflour
1 tablespoon dry sherry
1 tablespoon soy sauce
zest of 1 orange and 1 lemon, blanched
½ cup fresh orange juice
3 tablespoons lemon juice
1 teaspoon honey

chilli-peanut noodles
¼ cup pure peanut butter
¼ cup peanut oil
1 tablespoon Chinese chilli oil
1 tablespoon rice vinegar
1 tablespoon soy sauce
½ teaspoon honey
250 g Chinese noodles, cooked and drained

toasted sesame and chilli oils to serve
fresh coriander leaves and sprouts to garnish

Rinse the calamari and dry well. Mix with the oil, ginger, garlic and spring onions. Stir-fry in a wok or wide pan over a fierce heat for a few minutes or until just cooked and tender.

Whisk together the ingredients for the sauce. Pour in the sauce and stir until thick and smooth. Check seasoning and add salt if necessary.

Mix together the ingredients for the noodles.

Serve the calamari over the chilli-peanut noodles and garnish with coriander and sprouts. Pass around toasted sesame and chilli oils.

chinese-style pork with braised shiitake mushrooms and noodles

for 4

about 500 g slim pork fillet

marinade
½ cup soy sauce
1 tablespoon brown sugar
2 tablespoons dry sherry
2 tablespoons tomato ketchup
1 tablespoon lemon juice
2 cloves crushed garlic
1 large chunk ginger, peeled and crushed

mushrooms
12–16 dried shiitake mushrooms
1 tablespoon peanut oil
2 tablespoons Japanese soy sauce
1 tablespoon dry sherry
4 tablespoons sweet white wine
200 g Chinese egg noodles
1–2 tablespoons sesame oil
fresh coriander leaves

steamed tenderstem broccoli to serve

Combine the marinade ingredients, and marinate the pork overnight, turning once or twice. Roast, uncovered, at 180°C for 45 minutes, basting now and again, until cooked through but still moist.

Soak the mushrooms in hot water for half an hour. Drain, reserving one cup of liquid. Cut out the tough stems. Heat the oil and add the mushrooms. Stir-fry for a minute or two. Pour in the reserved mushroom liquid, sherry and wine. Bring to a bubble, then reduce the heat and simmer for about 15 minutes or until succulent and tender.

Cook the noodles according to package instructions. Drain well and add to the pan of mushrooms. Add the sesame oil and mix well together. Heat through and sprinkle with coriander leaves. Check seasoning.

Slice the pork thinly and serve with the mushrooms and noodles and broccoli.

FROM NIGELLA LAWSON, THAT FABULOUS ENGLISH COOKERY WRITER, I'VE LEARNT THE ART OF BRAISING SHIITAKE MUSHROOMS, PLUS MUCH MORE FROM HER BOOK *HOW TO EAT* (CHATTO AND WINDUS)

chinese-style duck and pancakes with plum sauce

for 4 – 6

2 duck breasts, about 200 g each
peanut oil
1–2 teaspoons five-spice powder

pancakes
1½ cups flour
1 cup boiling water
sesame oil

matchsticks of cucumber and spring onion and
bottled Chinese plum sauce to serve

Cut each breast in half lengthwise. Pour over boiling water, then dry well. Separate the meat from the skin and remove any fat. Prick the skin all over and score on both sides. Moisten the meat lightly with oil and rub with five-spice powder. Slide under a preheated grill and cook until the meat is firm to the touch but still moist and slightly pink. The skin will take longer to crisp and brown. Slice the meat and skin across.

To make the pancakes, place the flour in a bowl and pour over the boiling water. Mix well with a wooden spoon and knead for a few minutes, dusting with flour if the mixture seems too sticky. Roll into a log, cover with a damp cloth and leave for half an hour. Slice across thinly and pat or roll out into small rounds (makes about 24). Cook in a barely oiled non-stick pan until lightly spotted. Serve at room temperature or reheat in the microwave.

Spread the pancakes with plum sauce and fill with duck, skin, cucumber and spring onion. Wrap up and eat in the hand. Chinese-style roast pork (page 65) is also good wrapped in pancakes. And if there's no time to make pancakes, lettuce leaves make a good alternative wrap.

friday family favourites

GATHER THE KIDS ROUND
THE TABLE, BEFORE THEY
DISAPPEAR FOR THE
WEEKEND, AND LET EACH
MEMBER OF THE FAMILY, IN
TURN, CHOOSE THE MENU.
A GREAT MAIN COURSE
AND A SCRUMPTIOUS
PUDDING WILL WIN THE
COOK COMPLIMENTS AND
MAKE EVERYONE HAPPY.

spiced citrus chicken

for 6 – 8

12 chicken thighs
1 small onion, chopped
½ teaspoon ground cinnamon
½ teaspoon ground cardamom
½ teaspoon turmeric
½ teaspoon paprika
3 tablespoons sunflower oil
rind and juice of 3 oranges
rind and juice of 1 lemon
1 cup chicken stock
1–2 tablespoons honey
salt and milled black pepper to taste

basmati rice and steamed baby squash

Wash, trim and dry the chicken portions. Season lightly. Pound the onion and spices together. Mix with the oil to form a paste and smear all over the chicken pieces and under the skin. Arrange in a single layer in a roasting pan coated with a non-stick cooking spray. Roast at 180°C for 45 minutes or until tender. Pour boiling water over the thinly sliced citrus rinds and drain. Simmer the blanched rinds in the stock and honey for about 10 minutes or until very tender. Mix together with the citrus juices and pour over the chicken. Cook for a further 10–15 minutes or until glazed and nicely browned. Season to taste and serve with basmati rice and a mix of steamed baby squash.

70

flat-roast chicken with feta and potatoes

for 4 - 6

1 large whole free-range chicken
250 g feta cheese
olive oil
basil leaves
lots of garlic, crushed
1 kg medium potatoes, scrubbed
and thinly sliced
1 onion, thinly sliced
1 or 2 lemons
salt and milled black pepper

spinach salad to serve

Using a strong pair of kitchen scissors, **cut out the backbone of the chicken** and the wing tips. (Freeze for broth.) Wash and dry the chicken well. Open out the chicken as flat as possible. Moisten the feta with olive oil and push under the skin along with basil leaves and crushed garlic. Season and oil all over. Arrange a layer of potatoes and sliced onion in a well-oiled roasting pan. Add lots of crushed garlic, some seasoning and oil. Place the chicken on top. Squeeze over lemon juice. Roast at 200°C for an hour or until nicely browned and crisp, and both the chicken and potatoes are tender. Serve with a salad of dressed tender spinach leaves.

seven-hour lamb

for 6

2 kg leg of lamb
2–3 tablespoons olive oil
1–2 heads garlic, halved across
200 g shallots, skinned, or
1 or 2 sliced onions
sprigs of fresh rosemary

1 cup beef or chicken stock
1 cup dry red wine
salt and milled black pepper

mashed potatoes, lentils
and rocket salad to serve

Trim any excess fat from lamb, season and moisten with oil. Place garlic, shallots, onions and rosemary in an oiled heavy casserole just large enough to take the lamb. Add lamb and pour over the stock and wine. Cover with 1–2 sheets of oiled greaseproof paper and then cover with a tight-fitting lid. Bake at 120°C for 7 hours or until meltingly tender. Cut with a spoon and serve with mashed potatoes, lentils and plenty of gravy, and a side salad of rocket leaves. Alternatively, remove lamb and keep warm while reducing cooking liquids on top of the stove to a saucy consistency.

baked sole with italian cheeses and vegetable pasta

for 4

4 soles, about 1 kg
1 lemon
1 free-range egg, separated
1 cup freshly grated Italian Parmesan
¼ cup soft ricotta cheese
salt and milled black pepper

pasta

350 g tiny pasta
350 g mixed diced or shredded
fresh vegetables
2 tablespoons olive oil
1 cup cream
1 fat clove garlic, crushed
2 tablespoons chopped Italian parsley
or shredded basil leaves

IF FRESH ANGEL
FISH IS
AVAILABLE, IT
MAKES A GOOD
SUBSTITUTE
FOR SOLE.

Have soles skinned and trimmed. Wash and dry well and arrange in a single layer in an oiled roasting pan. Season lightly and squeeze over some lemon juice. Whisk the egg white with a little salt until stiff but not dry. Whisk in lightly beaten egg yolk, then mix in cheeses. Add a grinding of black pepper. Smear the paste over the soles and bake at 220°C for 10 minutes. If necessary, turn on the grill and cook for a minute or two, watching carefully, until speckled golden brown.

To prepare the pasta, cook until just tender. In a wide pan, stir-fry vegetables in the heated oil until crisp but tender. Pour in the cream, add some garlic and seasoning, and allow to bubble and reduce slightly. Mix into hot drained pasta.

Serve the fish with the creamy vegetable pasta.

braised brisket of beef

for 6 – 8

1.5–2 kg boned and rolled brisket of beef
2 tablespoons flour
2 tablespoons paprika
1 teaspoon salt
⅛ teaspoon black pepper
2 tablespoons sunflower oil
2 onions, thinly sliced
4 carrots, thinly sliced
2 sticks celery, thinly sliced
2 tablespoons tomato paste
2 bay leaves
12 cups water

Trim any excess fat from the beef.

Mix together the flour, paprika, salt and pepper, then roll the beef in it to coat evenly. Heat the oil in a heavy casserole on top of the stove. Add the beef and brown well. Remove and set aside. Reduce the heat and stir in the sliced vegetables, adding more oil if necessary. Cook gently until pale golden in colour, adding a little water if necessary to prevent sticking. Stir in the tomato paste. Return the meat to the casserole. Add the bay leaves and pour over the water to cover. Bring to the boil, cover tightly, then bake at 180°C for 1½ to 2 hours or until the meat is very tender. Remove the beef, skim off the fat from the cooking liquid and fish out the bay leaves. Reduce over a high heat to thicken slightly, then use a hand blender to purée the vegetables and thicken the sauce a little more. Check seasoning.

Serve the beef thinly sliced with lots of sauce, creamy mashed potatoes and lightly steamed cabbage with caraway.

roasted vegetables with polenta crust

for 6

1.5 kg roasted vegetables (see chopped
roasted vegetable salad page 43)
1 cup grated mozzarella
roasted tomato sauce (see goat cheese
macaroni page 53)
3 cups vegetable stock
1 cup instant polenta
½ cup grated Italian Parmesan
2 tablespoons butter
olive oil
salt and milled black pepper

Turn the chopped roasted vegetables
into an oiled baking dish. Sprinkle with
mozzarella and spoon over the tomato sauce.
Bring the stock to the boil, add the polenta
and cook, stirring all the time, until thick and
smooth. Remove from the heat and add half
the Parmesan, the butter and seasoning to
taste. Spread evenly over the vegetables,
sprinkle with the rest of the Parmesan and
drizzle with olive oil. Bake at 200°C for about
30 minutes or until golden.

IF THERE IS A NEED
TO CATER FOR
VEGETARIANS, THIS IS
A PERFECT OPTION.

for 8

150 g dark chocolate, broken into bits
100 g unsalted butter
1¼ cups flour
½ teaspoon baking powder
¼ teaspoon salt
¾ cup castor sugar
2 free-range eggs
100 g walnuts or pecan nuts, coarsely chopped

good quality vanilla ice cream and strawberries in season, and hot chocolate sauce (see page 82) to serve

Melt the chocolate with the butter. Stir together until smooth. Set aside to cool slightly. Sift the flour with the baking powder and salt. Gradually add the sugar and eggs to the melted chocolate mixture, beating together until smooth. Stir in the sifted flour mixture and the nuts. Turn into a buttered and non-stick, paper-lined pizza pan (about 26 cm in diameter). Bake at 180°C for 20 minutes or until a tester inserted comes out clean.

To serve, cut in wedges and top with ice cream, strawberries (when available) and a drizzle of hot chocolate sauce.

IT'S ONLY A GREAT
BIG CHOCOLATE
BROWNIE, BUT
SUCH A FUN WAY
OF PRESENTING IT.

frozen coffee tiramisu

for 12

4 free-range eggs, separated
½ cup castor sugar
2 tablespoons instant espresso coffee
¼ cup coffee liqueur
500 g fresh mascarpone
½ cup fresh cream, whipped
about 200 g Italian sponge fingers

about 1 cup freshly made strong coffee
cocoa for sprinkling
100 g dark chocolate for making shards

chocolate shards to garnish
coffee liqueur (optional) to serve

Beat the egg yolks with the castor sugar and the coffee until thick and creamy. Add the coffee liqueur. Beat in the mascarpone. Fold in the stiffly beaten egg whites and softly beaten cream. Line a large loaf pan with non-stick paper. Pour in a third of the mascarpone mixture. Add a layer of soaked biscuits (dip the sponge fingers in the hot coffee as you add them), then a third of the mascarpone mixture, another layer of biscuits, then the last of the mascarpone mixture. Press in a final layer of soaked biscuits. Freeze for at least 8 hours. Turn out, removing the paper. Sift over cocoa and decorate with shards of chocolate. If you like, pour coffee liqueur over each serving.

   To make the chocolate shards, melt the dark chocolate and spread thinly over a sheet of non-stick baking paper. Refrigerate to set, then break into shards and use to decorate.

TIRAMISU, THESE DAYS, IS AS COMMON AS GREEK SALAD. BUT THERE ARE GREEK SALADS AND THERE ARE GREEK SALADS, AND I BELIEVE THAT THIS VERSION OF TIRAMISU WARRANTS INCLUSION. THIS IS NOT A TRUE ICE-CREAM, BUT KNOWN AS 'SEMI-FREDDO', ITALIAN FOR HALF-COLD, BECAUSE THE DESSERT IS SIMPLY FROZEN IN A SUITABLE CONTAINER.

rolled pavlova

for 8 – 10

6 free-range egg whites
pinch cream of tartar
pinch salt
¾ cup castor sugar
1 tablespoon cornflour

filling

2 cups best ice cream
or 1 cup lemon curd mixed with 1 cup cream,
whipped

Butter a swiss-roll tin and line with a sheet of non-stick baking paper. Beat the egg whites until foamy, then beat in the cream of tartar and salt. Continue to beat until soft peaks form. Gradually beat in the castor sugar until very stiff and glossy, then beat in the cornflour. Turn into the prepared tin and smooth with a large spatula. Bake at 190°C for 10 minutes or until firm to the touch. Turn out onto a clean, damp tea towel covered with a sheet of non-stick baking paper. Remove the paper carefully, then spread with the filling and roll up gently, like a swiss roll, with the help of the paper and tea towel. Freeze until ready to serve, or refrigerate if using the lemon curd filling

EGG WHITES FREEZE BEAUTIFULLY. ONCE YOU'VE COLLECTED ENOUGH, USE THEM FOR THIS DELICIOUS DESSERT, FILLING IT EITHER WITH THE BEST QUALITY ICE CREAM – VANILLA, BUTTERSCOTCH OR BERRY ARE ALL GOOD – OR WITH A CREAMY LEMON CURD. KIDS AND TEENAGERS WILL LOVE THE FIRST, ADULTS (WELL, MOST OF THEM) WILL APPRECIATE THE JUXTAPOSITION OF SWEET AND TART.

baked vanilla custard with caramel and chocolate sauce

for 6 – 8

1 cup cream
1½ cups full cream milk
½ cup vanilla sugar (page 100)
9 free-range egg yolks
2 teaspoons vanilla

caramel sauce

½ cup sugar
⅓ cup water
½ cup cream

chocolate sauce

½ cup cream
100 g dark chocolate, broken into bits

Gently warm the cream, milk and sugar, stirring until the sugar has dissolved. Beat the egg yolks, then whisk in the lukewarm liquid and the vanilla. Strain into a 20 cm buttered flan or pie dish and place in a larger dish of hot water. Bake at 150°C for 1¼ hours or until set and a tester inserted comes out clean. Refrigerate overnight.

To make the caramel sauce, place the sugar and water in a small heavy saucepan and heat, stirring until the sugar dissolves. Boil until a good caramel colour, then remove from the heat and stir in the cream until blended and smooth.

To make the chocolate sauce, gently heat the cream and chocolate together and stir until smooth.

Top servings of custard with the two sauces and serve.

freeform fruit tart

for 8

cream cheese pastry	topping
90 g cold butter, cut into bits	fresh fruit in season
125 g cream cheese	cinnamon
1 cup flour	sugar
beaten egg white for brushing	butter
sugar for sprinkling	runny cream or thick yoghurt to serve

Process or knead together the butter, cream cheese and flour to form a ball. Coat lightly with flour and chill for an hour until firm enough to roll. Roll out to form a rectangle. Place on a buttered baking sheet. Tuck in the edges and press down with the tines of a fork. Brush all over with lightly beaten egg white and sprinkle with sugar.

Press in slices of any fresh fruit – apples, pears and plums are all good. Sprinkle generously with cinnamon and sugar and dot with bits of butter. Refrigerate until baking. Bake at 230°C for 20 minutes or until deeply browned. Serve while still warm with runny cream or thick Greek yoghurt.

THIS QUICK-TO-MAKE DELICIOUS PASTRY IS A BASE FOR ANY FRUITS IN SEASON.

saturday
sophisticated dinners
for good friends

THIS IS THE NIGHT TO ENJOY
LOVELY FOOD, FINE WINE AND
GOOD TALK. PLAN AND SHOP
AHEAD OF TIME. MAKE THE
DISHES YOU LOVE OR THE
ONES YOU ARE DYING TO TRY.
PRETTY UP THE TABLE AND
LEAVE ENOUGH TIME TO DO
THE SAME FOR YOURSELF.

baked ricotta with marinated baby vegetables

for 8

1 kg fresh ricotta
3 free-range eggs, separated
⅓ cup grated Parmesan
salt and milled pepper

marinated baby vegetables
500–700 g assorted baby vegetables
(fennel, marrows, squash, cabbage,
cauliflower, asparagus and green beans)
½ cup white wine vinegar
½ cup olive oil
1 clove garlic, smashed
a few sprigs thyme and rosemary
1 teaspoon coriander seeds
1 teaspoon salt
½ teaspoon black peppercorns

crusty bread to serve

Beat the ricotta with the egg yolks until smooth. Stir in the Parmesan and seasoning to taste. Beat the egg whites until stiff, then fold into the ricotta mixture. Coat a 23 cm springform pan with non-stick cooking spray. Pour in the beaten mixture, smoothing the top. Bake at 190°C for about an hour or until well risen, golden and firm. It will sink as it cools. Serve either warm or at room temperature, in wedges, with the marinated baby vegetables.

To make the marinated baby vegetables, drop vegetables into a saucepan of salted boiling water. Allow to return to the boil, then drain well. Place in a heatproof glass bowl. Simmer the marinade ingredients together for a minute or two, then immediately pour over the vegetables and mix together.

roasted celery hearts with parmesan and anchovies

for 4

4 celery hearts (use the rest in soups,
stocks and casseroles)
4 tablespoons olive oil
100 g shaved Italian Parmesan
1 x can or small bottle anchovies

Place the celery hearts in an oiled baking pan and moisten with the olive oil. Season lightly. Roast at 200°C for an hour, turning halfway, or until tender. Top with shavings of cheese and bits of anchovy. Return to the oven for a few minutes until the cheese has melted. Serve immediately.

HERE ARE FIVE GREAT STARTERS, BUT DON'T FORGET TO REFER TO THE OTHER CHAPTERS FOR IDEAS. VIETNAMESE SPRING ROLLS, PERHAPS, A SMALL PORTION OF ONE OF THE SALADS, OR SOUP ON A COLD NIGHT. AND OF COURSE ANY OF THE NIBBLES SUGGESTED FOR SUNDAY.

salmon tartare

for 4

200–250 g very fresh Norwegian
salmon, filleted
6–8 slim salad onions, finely chopped
1 tablespoon capers, rinsed, dried
and finely chopped
2 tablespoons pickled gherkins, finely chopped
1 tablespoon lemon juice
2 tablespoons chopped parsley
2 tablespoons thick mayonnaise
salt and milled black pepper

crème fraîche and hot toast to serve
red salmon roe or chives to garnish

Chop the salmon and mix with the onions, capers, gherkins, lemon juice, parsley and mayonnaise. Add salt and pepper to taste. Pack into small ramekins, or into small, tall moulds if you intend inverting them to serve. Either way, top with blobs of crème fraîche and garnish with salmon roe or chives. Serve with hot toast.

USE THE BEST QUALITY
FRESH FISH, BUT IF
YOU PREFER,
SUBSTITUTE WITH
SMOKED SALMON.

88

green asparagus with quail eggs and caper sauce

for 6

500–600 g thick, fresh green asparagus
12 quail eggs, hard-boiled

caper sauce
1 cup thick home-made mayonnaise
¾ cup crème fraîche
1 tablespoon strained lemon juice
2 tablespoons salted capers, well rinsed,
dried and chopped
milled black pepper to taste

grissini to serve

Trim and lightly peel the asparagus.
Drop into a large saucepan of salted boiling water. Allow to return to the boil. Check one asparagus. It should be bright green and tender but crisp. Drain and cover with ice.
   Mix together all the ingredients for the caper sauce.
   Use a platter or individual plates for serving. Start with the caper sauce, then add the asparagus and garnish with halved hard-boiled quail eggs. Serve with grissini.

GENTLY ADD QUAIL EGGS
TO BOILING WATER AND
COOK FOR 2–3 MINUTES.

poached fish in chunky tomato sauce

for 6

1 kg mixed fish, filleted and cut
into large chunks

chunky tomato sauce
1 onion, chopped
1 leek, well-washed and thinly sliced
3–4 tablespoons olive oil
2 sticks celery, chopped
1 large fennel bulb, chopped
(or use more leeks)
3 fat cloves garlic, crushed
½–1 teaspoon crushed chilli
½–1 teaspoon saffron threads
1 x 410 g tin tomatoes, crushed
1 bay leaf
strip of orange rind, blanched
juice of 1 orange
½ cup dry white wine
½ cup water or fish stock
2 tablespoons chopped Italian parsley

oven-toasted ciabatta (see soups page 39) or
tiny pasta mixed with shredded, blanched
spinach, and garlic-flavoured, thick
home-made mayonnaise to serve
Italian parsley or basil leaves to garnish

To make the sauce, gently cook the onion and leek in olive oil for 5–10 minutes, stirring now and again, until very soft but still pale. Add the celery and fennel, continue to cook gently until softened. Stir in garlic and seasoning. Add the crushed chilli and saffron. Cook for a minute or two longer. Add tomatoes and bay leaf and simmer for 5–10 minutes, stirring now and again. Add the orange zest, juice, wine and water or stock, and bring to a bubble. Cover and simmer for about 20 minutes. Add the fish and poach for 5 minutes or until just cooked. Stir in the parsley and check seasoning.

To serve, centre a slice of toast or a big spoonful of pasta in large shallow bowls or deep plates. Ladle over the fish and sauce and top with mayonnaise. Garnish with herbs.

MADE-TO-REMEMBER MAIN
COURSES ARE NOT THE SORT
TO PALE BETWEEN A STUNNING
STARTER AND FABULOUS DESSERT.

SATURDAY

sesame roast quail with coconut rice

for 8

8 quail	1 teaspoon five-spice powder
sesame seeds	
	coconut rice
marinade	1½ cups Thai fragrant rice
4 tablespoons honey	1 x 400 ml tin coconut cream
8 tablespoons soy sauce	½ cup water
4 tablespoons dry sherry	1 lemongrass heart, bruised
4 tablespoons peanut oil	1 teaspoon salt
4 tablespoons sesame oil	
1–2 fat cloves garlic, crushed	coriander leaves to garnish
1 chunk peeled ginger, grated	

Always **defrost quail** slowly in the refrigerator. Rinse the birds and spatchcock by cutting out the backbone with a pair of kitchen scissors, then flattening them with the palm of the hand. Coat a large, shallow roasting pan with a non-stick cooking spray. Add the quails and pour over the marinade, turning the quails around to moisten all over. Leave for an hour or two, or overnight in the fridge. Arrange in a single layer skin-side up and sprinkle with sesame seeds. Roast at 230°C for 15 minutes or until nicely browned and just cooked through.

   To make the coconut rice, wash the rice well and drain. Place in a suitably sized heavy or non-stick saucepan. Pour in the coconut cream. Pour the half cup of water into the empty tin before adding to the rice. Add lemongrass and salt. Bring to the boil over medium heat, then cover and reduce the heat to low. Cook for 15 minutes, by which time all the liquid should be absorbed and the rice tender. Remove from the heat and allow to stand, still covered, before serving.

   Serve the roasted quail with the coconut rice, garnished with fresh coriander leaves.

oven-roasted prawns with mango salsa and green rice

for 4

500 g large prawns, unshelled but deveined
⅓ cup olive oil
1 teaspoon curry powder
1 tablespoon finely chopped parsley
2 fat cloves garlic, crushed
2 tablespoons lemon juice
salt and milled pepper
fresh basil and coriander leaves to garnish

mango salsa
1 ripe mango, peeled and diced
3 spring onions, finely chopped
1 fresh red chilli, finely chopped
2 tablespoons lemon juice
2 tablespoons chopped coriander leaves
2 tablespoons shredded basil leaves
salt and milled pepper

green basmati rice
2 cups freshly cooked basmati rice
¼ cup chopped spring onions
¼ cup chopped fresh coriander leaves
¼ teaspoon ground coriander
¼ teaspoon ground cumin
1 tablespoon olive oil
salt and milled pepper

Arrange the prawns in a single layer in a roasting pan. Pour over the olive oil and roast at 230°C for 5 minutes, then turn. Meanwhile, mix together the curry powder, parsley, garlic and lemon juice. Spread over the prawns. Roast for another 3–5 minutes or until the prawns are pink and curled. Add seasoning to taste.

Mix together all the ingredients for the salsa.

Mix together all the ingredients for the rice.

Serve the oven-roasted prawns with the mango salsa and green basmati rice. Garnish with basil and coriander leaves.

crispy duck with red wine sauce and roasted pears and potatoes

for 4

1 duck, about 2 kg, cleaned
salt and milled pepper
4 firm pears, peeled, cored and
quartered lengthwise
4 potatoes, peeled and quartered lengthwise
sprigs of thyme

red wine sauce
duck liver
2 tablespoons sunflower oil
giblets, cleaned and chopped
1 onion, chopped
1 clove garlic, crushed
1 cinnamon stick
a few sprigs thyme
3 tablespoons sugar
⅓ cup red wine vinegar
1 cup port
1 cup red wine
3 cups chicken stock
salt and peppercorns

watercress or chicory (or both) to garnish

Pour boiling water over the duck. Drain. Prick the skin all over. Season inside and out. Insert a vertical roaster and place in a large baking pan. Leave in a cool place to dry the skin or use a hair dryer to hasten the process. Roast at 220°C for 30 minutes. Remove from the oven. Pour off the fat. Reduce the oven temperature to 180°C. Return the duck to the pan and add the pears and potatoes in a single layer around the duck. Tuck in thyme. Roast for 1–1½ hours, turning the pears and potatoes once or twice, until all is tender and the duck skin is crisp and deeply browned.

To make the red wine sauce, brown the duck liver in 1 tablespoon of oil. Remove and set aside. In the same saucepan brown the giblets, adding the rest of the oil. Add the onion and cook until tender. Add the garlic, cinnamon stick, thyme and sugar. Stir until the sugar melts. Pour in the vinegar and boil until almost evaporated. Pour in the port, wine and stock. Season and simmer for about 1 hour or until reduced by half. Strain. Before serving, reheat with the chopped liver. If necessary, reduce sauce again to thicken and intensify the flavour. Check seasoning.

slow-roasted lamb shanks with quick leek risotto

for 6

	leek risotto
6 lamb shanks	1 bunch leeks, well washed and thinly sliced
¼ cup fresh lemon juice	2–3 tablespoons olive oil
½ cup olive oil	1½ cups risotto rice
4–6 fat cloves garlic, crushed	3 cups chicken broth
3–4 sprigs rosemary	salt and milled black pepper to taste
salt and milled black pepper	2–3 tablespoons chopped Italian parsley

mixed greens to serve

Trim any excess fat from the lamb, season and place in a giant-sized cooking bag. Mix together the rest of the ingredients and pour into the bag. Knot to seal. Leave to marinate in the fridge for about 2 days, turning occasionally. To cook, place the bag in a roasting pan. Prick the bag and roast at 160°C for 4 hours, turning halfway, or until meltingly tender and starting to fall off the bone.

   To make the risotto, soften the leeks in the heated oil. Add the rice and stir until coated. Pour in the broth and bring to a simmer. Stir in salt, cover and cook for 20 minutes or until the liquid is absorbed and the rice tender. Stir in the parsley and check seasoning.

   Serve the lamb with quick risotto and a tangle of steamed greens.

sliced fresh fruits with lemon rum syrup

syrup	fresh fruits
1 cup water	strips of lemon peel
2 cups sugar	juice of half a lemon, strained
1 stick cinnamon	3 tablespoons white rum
2 cloves or 2 star anise	
	fresh mint to garnish

Boil the water, sugar, spices and lemon peel together for about 5 minutes to form a syrup. Stir only until the sugar dissolves. Add the strained lemon juice and the rum to the syrup. Allow to cool. The syrup keeps well in a sealed jar in the refrigerator.

Slice and arrange fruits on a platter or individual plates, then moisten with the syrup and chill until serving. Decorate with fresh mint.

SELECT ANY OF THE FRESH FRUITS IN SEASON – WHATEVER LOOKS GOOD AND TASTES GOOD TOGETHER.

SATURDAY

grilled sugared plums with berries

for 6

12 plums, halved and stoned
2 tablespoons vanilla sugar (page 100)

sauce
250 g red berries (raspberries or strawberries)
2 tablespoons vanilla sugar
juice of 1 orange

fresh berries and mint to garnish

Arrange the plums in a single layer in a buttered ovenproof pan. Sprinkle with the sugar and slide under a hot grill until the sugar starts to bubble.

To make the sauce, blend the berries, vanilla sugar and orange juice, then strain.

Pour some berry sauce into a bowl. Add the plums and garnish with berries and mint.

roasted **strawberries**

for 6 – 8

800 g large strawberries, hulled
½ cup vanilla sugar

mascarpone or good vanilla ice cream, and
vanilla liqueur to serve

Line a roasting pan with non-stick greaseproof baking paper. Arrange the strawberries in a single layer. Sprinkle with the vanilla sugar. Roast at 180°C for half an hour. Serve warm with mascarpone or ice cream. Add a splash of vanilla liqueur.

BURY VANILLA PODS IN A JAR
OF SUGAR. THE PODS WILL
KEEP WELL AND IMPART
THEIR FLAVOUR TO THE
SUGAR. KEEP THE JAR
TOPPED UP WITH SUGAR

roasted pears with apricots and citrus ice

for 4

lemon or orange ice	**pears**
	60 g unsalted butter
apricots	4 firm ripe pears
125 g dried apricots	¼ cup sugar
strips of orange peel	
brandy to cover	

Pour boiling water over the apricots and peel, then drain. Pack into a small jar and pour over enough brandy to cover. Leave overnight or longer.

To roast the pears, heat the butter in a heavy ovenproof pan on top of the stove. Add the quartered and cored pears and sauté for a few minutes until golden. Sprinkle with the sugar and roast at 230°C for 20 minutes or until golden brown and tender. Serve with the brandied apricots and scoops of lemon or orange ice.

chocolate walnut tart

for 8

**20 cm half-baked pastry shell
(see sweet pastry recipe page 126)**

**filling
200 g walnuts
75–100 g dark chocolate
60 g unsalted butter
¼ cup sugar
½ cup cream
1 tablespoon honey**

Roast the walnuts for about 10 minutes in the oven preheated to 180°C, then chop coarsely. Spread the cooled pastry shell with a thin layer of melted chocolate. Melt the butter in a suitable saucepan. Stir in the sugar, cream and honey. Bring to a boil, stirring until the sugar has dissolved. Allow to boil for 2 minutes until reduced and caramel-coloured. Stir in the chopped nuts, then turn into the chocolate-lined tart shell. Bake at 180°C for 20 minutes or until golden. Remelt the remaining chocolate and drizzle over the cooled tart.

DEPENDING ON HOW THINLY THE PASTRY MIXTURE IS ROLLED, IT CAN BE USED TO FILL ONE OR TWO LOOSE-BOTTOMED 20 CM TART TINS, ONE MEDIUM 23 CM TIN OR ONE LARGE 28 CM TIN.

102

lazy sunday lunches

SUNDAY LUNCH, ESPECIALLY ON COLD DAYS IN WINTER, IS A RELAXING WAY TO SEE FRIENDS. I LIKE A GENEROUS MAIN COURSE, HOMEY NOT HAUTE. PUT OUT NIBBLES TO START. AS IT IS GENERALLY TEA-TIME WHEN DESSERT COMES UP, A CAKE IS PERFECT. FOR SUMMER LUNCHES, ON A COOL TERRACE OR NEXT TO THE POOL, HERE'S AN EXCELLENT CHICKEN SALAD OR A ROASTED FISH DISH SERVED AT ROOM TEMPERATURE.

SUNDAY

polenta and ricotta **pizzas**

for 10 – 12

400 g ricotta
basil pesto (page 119)
Parmesan shavings

topping
bright peppers
baby tomatoes or sundried tomatoes
anchovies or slices of salami
olives
crushed garlic
origanum
salt and milled black pepper
olive oil

fresh basil to garnish

Coat a pizza pan (20–25 cm in diameter) with a non-stick cooking spray. Mash about 400 g ricotta into a round to fit the pan. Spread with a layer of basil pesto and shavings of Parmesan. Top with strips of bright peppers, halved baby tomatoes or strips of marinated sundried tomato, bits of anchovy or salami and olives. Smear with a little crushed garlic, if you like, and sprinkle with origanum. Season with a little salt and milled black pepper. Moisten with olive oil and bake at 190°C for 20–25 minutes. Garnish with fresh basil. If you like, serve at room temperature, cut into wedges to spread on crostini.

Do the same thing with polenta. Use the miraculously easy instant polenta and spread a layer in a well-oiled pizza pan. This time spread with sundried tomato pesto instead of the basil, add thinly sliced mozzarella, then proceed as above, adding a sprinkling of Parmesan. Cut into wedges, but eat on its own, straight from the oven.

106

hot roasted **nuts**

for 8

100 g unskinned almonds
100 g raw cashews
100 g pecans
100 g raw, giant red-skinned peanuts

Spread the nuts in a single layer on a baking tray. Roast at 180°C, turning once or twice, for 15–20 minutes, or until golden brown. Season with Maldon sea salt. If you like them spicy, sprinkle with some chilli powder. Serve while still warm.

marinated **olives**

for 8 – 10

1 cup drained olives, any kind or a mix
2 lemons, sliced and quartered
2 smashed garlic cloves

1 tablespoon coriander seeds, cracked
1 teaspoon dried origanum
olive oil to cover

Pack the ingredients into a jar, then cover with olive oil. Refrigerate for storing, but serve at room temperature. Strain leftover oil and use in a salad dressing.

quick cheese and tomato tart

for 12

8 sheets phyllo pastry
melted butter or olive oil
½ cup freshly grated Parmesan
1 cup grated mozzarella cheese
1 onion, thinly sliced
1 tablespoon chopped fresh origanum
6 large ripe red tomatoes, sliced
salt and milled black pepper
olive oil for drizzling

Brush a baking sheet with melted butter. Place a sheet of phyllo on it. Brush with melted butter and sprinkle with Parmesan. Repeat with the rest of the sheets of pastry. Sprinkle with the mozzarella and onion slices. Season lightly and sprinkle with the origanum. Cover with rows of overlapping tomato slices. Season and drizzle with oil. Bake at 200°C for 30–40 minutes or until crisp and golden. Cut into squares for serving.

108

crostini with salsa rosso or italian-style chopped liver

both toppings serve 6 – 8

crostini

sliced panini
olive oil for brushing
halved head of garlic

salsa rosso

4 firm ripe red tomatoes, chopped
1 small red onion, chopped
2 tablespoons chopped basil
3–4 tablespoons olive oil
salt and milled black pepper

italian-style chopped liver

250 g chicken livers
1 tablespoon olive oil
a sprig or two of rosemary
1 clove garlic, crushed
1 teaspoon balsamic vinegar
salt and milled black pepper

To make the crostini, toast the panini at 180°C for 10 minutes or until golden. Remove from the oven and brush with olive oil and rub with the halved head of garlic. Top the crostini with either the salsa rosso or the Italian-style chopped liver.

To make the salsa rosso, mix the ingredients together by hand.

To make the chopped liver, wash, trim and dry the livers. Heat the olive oil and the rosemary in a suitable pan. Add the livers and stir-fry until nicely browned but still moist and slightly pink inside. Stir in the garlic and vinegar and add seasoning to taste. Discard the rosemary and chop the livers by hand to a suitable consistency.

grilled aubergine spread with dukkah and toasted pita wedges

for 6 – 8

4 medium aubergines, about 1 kg
2 lemons
2 cloves garlic, crushed
2 tablespoons thick mayonnaise
2 tablespoons thick yoghurt
2 tablespoons olive oil
salt and milled black pepper to taste

dukkah
¼ cup sesame seeds
¼ cup chopped hazelnuts or almonds
3 tablespoons coriander seeds
2 tablespoons cumin seeds
½ teaspoon salt

a drizzle of olive oil and toasted pita wedges to serve

Prick the aubergines all over, then grill for about 20 minutes, turning now and again, until the skin is charred and the flesh soft. Peel the aubergines and cover with water to which the juice of one lemon and some salt has been added. Leave for about 10 minutes to help prevent discolouration. Drain and dry. Blend with the strained juice of the second lemon, the garlic, mayonnaise, yoghurt and seasoning to taste. Turn onto a platter and spread evenly. Refrigerate to firm. Before serving, sprinkle the aubergine spread with 2–3 tablespoons of dukkah, drizzle with oil, and serve with the toasted pita wedges.

To make the dukkah, dry-fry the sesame seeds and nuts in a pan on top of the stove for a few minutes, stirring all the time, until golden brown but not burnt. Dry-fry the coriander and cumin seeds until fragrant and starting to pop. Grind it all in a clean electric coffee grinder or special spice grinder. Add salt to taste and store in a sealed container in the refrigerator where it keeps well.

To make the toasted pita wedges, cut each pita bread across into 2 separate rounds; cut each round in half, and each half into 6 wedges. Dip a wide brush into olive oil mixed with origanum and seasoning and brush over wedges. Bake at 180°C for 10–15 minutes or until crisp and golden.

tropical chicken salad

for 6 – 8

8 skinned chicken breast fillets, about 800 g

marinade

2 teaspoons cumin seeds
3 cloves garlic, crushed
1 fresh red chilli, finely chopped
½ teaspoon salt
⅔ cup olive oil
3 tablespoons strained orange juice
3 tablespoons strained lemon juice
2 large firm ripe avocados, peeled and diced
2 large firm ripe mangos, peeled and diced
shelled pistachio nuts

dressing

1 cup sunflower oil
grated rind of 1 large bright orange
¾ cup strained orange juice
1 tablespoon honey
1 tablespoon soy sauce
salt and milled black pepper to taste

about 300 g mixed salad leaves to serve

Slash chicken pieces across 3 or 4 times. Stir-fry cumin seeds over medium heat for 2–3 minutes. Pound with garlic, chilli and salt to form a paste. Gently heat olive oil and mix with the paste until blended. Leave for 10 minutes, then beat in citrus juices. Mix with chicken and refrigerate, covered, for a few hours, or overnight. Sear the chicken on both sides on a hot, oiled grill pan. Do a few pieces at a time. Heat the remaining marinade and pour over the seared chicken. When cool, slice the chicken.

Blend together all the ingredients for the dressing.

To assemble, toss the greens with half the dressing. Check seasoning. Turn onto a platter. Top with sliced chicken, avocado and mango and spoon over the rest of the dressing. Sprinkle with nuts.

SUBSTITUTE SMALL PAPINOS WHEN MANGOES ARE NOT IN SEASON.

112

roasted butterflied chicken on polenta

for 4

1 medium whole free-range chicken,
butterflied
2–3 cloves garlic, crushed
3–4 cups polenta, cooked
10 thin slices proscuitto
fresh sage and rosemary
olive oil
milled salt and black pepper

pan-fried spinach leaves or
Swiss chard
to serve

Pat the washed chicken dry and season. Smear half the garlic on the underside of the chicken. Spread the polenta in an oiled roasting pan just large enough to take the chicken. Season and top with 6 slices ham, some sage and rosemary. Place the chicken on top, skin-side up. Lift the skin and smear the rest of the crushed garlic over the meat. Push in the rest of the ham over the breast. Moisten with olive oil and bake at 200°C for an hour or until crisp and golden. Serve with spinach leaves or Swiss chard, first blanched, then pan-fried in olive oil.

I'VE ONLY USED ONE CHICKEN IN THIS RECIPE, BUT IT'S EASY TO DOUBLE UP: SIMPLY USE A BIGGER ROASTING PAN

for 6

1 leg of lamb, about 2 kg, deboned and tied
bones from the leg
juice of 1 lemon
2 fat cloves garlic, crushed
1 teaspoon dried origanum
2 onions
2 x 410 g tins tomatoes, crushed
6 cups beef or chicken stock
350 g orzo (rice-shaped noodles)
½ cup grated Parmesan
100 g feta, cubed
salt and milled pepper

Season the lamb and flavour with the lemon juice, garlic and origanum. Halve and slice the onions into thin segments and place in the bottom of a lightly oiled roasting pan, together with the bones. Season lightly. Cover with a rack and place the lamb on top. Roast at 230°C for 15 minutes, then reduce the heat to 180°C. Pour the crushed tomatoes and 2 cups of the stock into the bottom of the roasting pan. Roast the lamb for an hour until nicely browned. Place the roast in a large ovenproof dish and leave to rest in the warm oven. Place the roasting pan on top of the stove, remove the bones, and pour in the remaining 4 cups stock. Bring to a boil, stirring all the time, to scrape the pan clean. Gradually stir in the orzo, then return to the oven, still at 180°C, for about 20 minutes or until the orzo is tender and plump with the absorbed liquid. Remove the lamb to carve and turn the orzo into the hot dish. Mix in the cheeses and check seasoning. Keep warm while carving the lamb. Return the sliced lamb and juices to the baking dish of orzo. Serve immediately.

for 10

10 portions skinned and filleted fish

marinade

1 cup olive oil
½ cup strained lemon juice
1 cup chopped coriander leaves
4–6 fat cloves garlic, crushed
1 tablespoon paprika
2 teaspoons ground cumin
½ teaspoon crushed chilli
salt to taste

spicy broth

¼ cup olive oil
1 large onion, chopped
4–6 sticks celery, chopped
4–6 fat cloves garlic, crushed
2 teaspoons crushed red chilli
2 teaspoons ground cumin
½ teaspoon ground coriander
1 tablespoon paprika
1 or 2 cinnamon sticks
1 x 410 g tin tomatoes, chopped
4 cups fish or vegetable stock
salt and milled pepper
500 g instant couscous

Blend together marinade ingredients. Mix the fish portions (about 150–200 g each) with the marinade and leave for a few hours or overnight in the fridge. Roast at 230°C for 5–10 minutes or until just cooked and still moist.

To make the spicy broth, heat the oil in a large saucepan. Add the onion and celery with a pinch of salt, and cook gently, covered, until softened but not browned. Stir in the garlic and spices, and cook for a minute or two. Add the tomatoes and cook for about 5 minutes. Pour in the stock and bring to a bubble, then simmer uncovered for 10 minutes. Check seasoning.

To serve, prepare the couscous according to packet instructions. Pile the hot, steamed couscous into a large bowl. Put out a bowl of piping hot broth and a platter of just-roasted fish, garnished with coriander leaves, if you wish. Use large, shallow pasta bowls for serving. Ladle lots of spicy broth over each helping of fish and couscous.

SUNDAY

117

roasted marinated fish with green vegetables

for 6 – 8

1 whole fresh fish, 2–2.5 kg, separated into
2 large fillets

marinade

juice of 2 oranges
juice of 2 lemons
1 fat clove garlic, crushed
1 tablespoon balsamic vinegar
¼ cup olive oil
1 teaspoon dried origanum or 1 tablespoon
chopped fresh origanum
salt and milled pepper to taste

vegetables

250 g slim green beans, trimmed
250 g slim green asparagus or 250 g slim
courgettes, slit lengthwise
200 g mangetout or sugar snap peas, trimmed
rocket leaves
olive oil

garlic mayonnaise, and roasted potato and
rosemary salad (see Monday's roasted
potato wedges on page 16) to serve

Mix together the marinade ingredients. Arrange the washed and dried fish fillets, side by side, in an oiled roasting pan. If you like, you can spray it with a non-stick cooking spray or line it with non-stick baking paper. Pour over the marinade and leave to stand at room temperature while heating the oven to 230°C. Roast for about 15 minutes until opaque, just firm to the touch and still moist. The cooking time varies according to the thickness of the fish, so take care not to overcook. Carefully lift the fish onto a platter and pour over any juices in the roasting pan. Add the green vegetables, steamed for about 10 minutes or until just cooked. Tuck in some rocket leaves and drizzle with a little olive oil.

Serve the fish at room temperature, with garlic mayonnaise and a roasted potato and rosemary salad.

Follow instructions on page 16 and dress the roasted potato wedges with olive oil, balsamic vinegar and crushed garlic. Serve at room temperature.

118

garlic mayonnaise

for 6 – 8

1 free-range egg
1 tablespoon strained lemon juice or
wine vinegar
salt and pepper
1 teaspoon mustard, dry or prepared
(optional)
1 cup sunflower oil
1–4 cloves garlic, crushed (optional)

It's a cinch to make the garlic mayonnaise with an electric hand blender. First blend the egg with the lemon juice, a little seasoning and mustard. Then, with the blender working all the time, gradually add the oil until thick and smooth. If too thick, blend in a little boiling water which also gives a satiny finish. Lastly, blend in the garlic, as much as you like.

basil pesto

2 cups fresh basil leaves, tightly packed
2 fat cloves garlic, crushed
¼ cup roasted pine nuts (or roasted sunflower
or pumpkin seeds)
⅔ cup olive oil
¾ cup Italian Parmesan, freshly grated
salt and pepper

Pound together, until well blended, the basil, garlic and pine nuts. Gradually add olive oil to make a thick paste. Mix in Parmesan by hand and add seasoning to taste.

BASIL PESTO MIXED WITH MAYONNAISE MAKES A GOOD ALTERNATIVE TO A CITRUSY MARINADE

SUNDAY

119

yoghurt and lemon syrup cake

for 8

½ cup self-raising flour
1 teaspoon baking powder
1¼ cups semolina
¾ cup castor sugar
⅔ cup sunflower oil
¾ cup Greek yoghurt
3 free-range eggs
grated rind and juice of 1 large lemon

syrup

¾ cup castor sugar
1 cup water
grated rind of 2 large lemons

Greek yoghurt and fresh berries to serve

Sift flour with baking powder. Stir in semolina and sugar. Beat together oil, yoghurt and eggs. Add rind and lemon juice. Gradually mix into flour mixture, then beat until smooth. Turn into a 20 cm springform pan coated with non-stick cooking spray. Bake at 190°C for 45 minutes or until a tester inserted comes out clean. Allow cake to cool for 5 minutes before removing to a serving plate.

To make the syrup, mix the ingredients in a small, heavy saucepan. Stir to dissolve the sugar, then allow to simmer undisturbed for 15 minutes or until reduced and syrupy. Prick cake all over and gradually spoon over syrup.

Cut in wedges and serve with yoghurt and berries.

cinnamon and brown sugar meringue torte

for 10 – 12

6 egg whites, at room temperature
1 teaspoon cream of tartar
1½ cups treacle sugar
2 teaspoons ground cinnamon

for the filling

2 cups cream
1 teaspoon ground cinnamon
100 g dark chocolate, chopped
100 g roasted pecans, chopped
100 g fresh dates, chopped
2 tablespoons rum

to serve

sifted icing sugar and cinnamon

Using electric beaters, beat the egg whites with the cream of tartar until soft peaks form. Gradually beat in the sugar and cinnamon, then continue beating for 5–10 minutes or until very stiff and glossy. Trace 4 x 20 cm circles onto non-stick baking paper. Using a spatula, cover the circles with meringue, smoothing evenly. Bake at 120°C for 3 hours. Turn off the heat and leave the meringue to cool in the oven for at least 2 hours, or overnight.

To make the filling, whip the cream with the cinnamon until stiff enough to hold its shape. Mix with the chocolate, nuts, dates and rum. Sandwich the meringue layers, with the filling in between. Refrigerate if made ahead of time.

To serve, dust with sifted icing sugar and cinnamon.

panforte

for 12 – 15

100 g blanched almonds, flaked

100 g walnuts or hazelnuts

¾ cup flour

¼ cup cocoa powder

½ teaspoon salt

½ teaspoon baking powder

½ teaspoon ground cloves

½ teaspoon grated nutmeg

½ teaspoon ground cinnamon

½ cup sugar

½ cup honey

⅔ cup water

½ cup mixed candied peel, chopped

¼ cup preserved or glacé orange, finely chopped

¼ cup preserved or glacé fig, finely chopped

¼ cup preserved or glacé melòn, finely chopped

icing sugar and cinnamon for sprinkling

Lightly toast the nuts in the oven at 180°C for about 10 minutes. If using hazelnuts rub off the skins, while still warm, using a tea towel. Sift together the flour, cocoa, salt, baking powder and spices. Mix together the sugar, honey and water in a saucepan. Cook over a low heat, stirring constantly, until the mixture boils. Simmer uncovered for a few minutes. Remove from the heat and beat into the flour mixture until very smooth. Mix in the nuts and fruits. Line a well-buttered or oiled 20 cm layer tin with rice paper. Bake at 160°C for an hour and 10 minutes, or until a tester inserted comes out clean. Allow to cool before turning out. Invert onto a plate and dust with sifted icing sugar and cinnamon. Store, wrapped in foil in an airtight tin. Slice thinly for serving.

A SPICY FRUIT AND NUT CAKE THAT ORIGINATES IN SIENNA. I BAKE MANY VARIATIONS OF THIS WONDERFUL CAKE, BUT FINALLY DECIDED TO INCLUDE THIS ONE.

warm chocolate cake

for 8

300 g dark chocolate, broken into bits
¼ cup coffee liqueur
¼ cup freshly made espresso coffee
5 free-range eggs
⅓ cup castor sugar
1 cup cream, whipped

coffee ice cream to serve

Coat a 23 cm springform pan, about 5 cm deep, with a non-stick cooking spray. Melt the chocolate over hot water (or in the microwave). Gently heat the coffee liqueur and espresso, then pour into the chocolate, without stirring. Beat the eggs and sugar relentlessly until thick, pale and fluffy. Add a quarter of it to the chocolate mixture, mixing well, then fold the chocolate mixture into the rest of the beaten egg mixture. Fold in the whipped cream. Pour into the prepared cake tin and place in a larger baking tin with enough hot water to come halfway up the sides. Bake at 180°C for an hour or until set. Allow to cool for 10 minutes before removing from the tin. Serve while still warm with scoops of good coffee ice cream.

apricot **almond tart**

for 8

sweet tart pastry

1½ cups flour

pinch salt

100 g cold unsalted butter

3 tablespoons icing sugar

1 free-range egg yolk

1 tablespoon iced water

1 tablespoon brandy

1 tablespoon oil

filling

½ cup ground almonds

1 tablespoon flour

60g soft butter

3 tablespoons sugar

1 free-range egg, beaten

pinch salt

1 tablespoon Amaretto liqueur

topping

350 g firm ripe apricots, halved

¼ cup flaked almonds

melted butter

sugar for sprinkling

Sift flour and salt into a bowl. Cut or grate in butter and rub lightly together with fingertips until crumbly. Sift in icing sugar. Beat egg yolk with water, brandy and oil. Pour into centre of flour mixture and mix together with a fork. Knead very lightly until mixture forms a ball, or mix in a food processor, taking care not to overprocess. Cover pastry and allow to rest in refrigerator before rolling out between 2 sheets of non-stick baking paper. Use to fill 1 medium 23 cm tart tin. Freeze any leftover pastry. Prick pastry shell all over, then freeze while heating oven to 190°C. To prevent shrinkage, fill with non-stick baking paper and dried beans. Bake for 15 minutes or until light brown. Remove paper and beans and bake for another 5 minutes. Allow to cool.

Mix together the filling ingredients. Fill the cooled, half-baked tart with the filling, spreading it evenly. Arrange the apricot halves, cut-side down, over filling. Tuck in the flaked almonds. Brush with butter and sprinkle lightly with sugar. Bake at 190°C for 35–45 minutes or until slightly puffed and set. Allow tart to cool a bit before removing from the tin. Serve while still warm, or cooled to room temperature.

in**dex**

128

conversion table
1 cup = 250 ml
1 tablespoon = 15 ml
1 teaspoon = 5 ml